María del Carmen Sillato
with the participation of Chary Sillato

Dialogues of Love against the Silence

Memories of Prison, Dreams of Freedom

Translated by
Y. L. Mariela Wong

Edited by
Issac Gabriel Salgado

Dialogues of Love against the Silence: Memories of Prison, Dreams of Freedom

ISBN-13: 978-1-952336-13-3
ISBN-10: 1-952336-13-9

Design and Layout: © Valeria Luján Lossada
Editor in chief: Carlos Velasquez Torres
E-mail: carlos@artepoetica.com
Mail: 38-38 215 Place, Bayside, NY 11361, USA.

©Dialogues of Love against the Silence: Memories of Prison, Dreams of Freedom, 2022 Escribana Books

All rights reserved. No part of this publication may be reproduced, distributed, or transmitted in any form or by any means, including photocopying, recording, or other electronic or mechanical methods, without the prior written permission of the publisher, except in the case of brief quotations embodied in critical reviews and certain other noncommercial uses permitted by copyright law. For permission requests, write to the publisher, addressed "Attention: Permissions Coordinator," at the address below: 38-38 215 Place, Bayside, NY 11361, USA

Todos los derechos reservados. Esta publicación no puede ser reproducida, ni en todo ni en parte, ni registrada en o transmitida por, un sistema de recuperación de información, en ninguna forma ni por ningún medio, sea mecánico, fotoquímico, electrónico, magnético, electroóptico, por fotocopia, o cualquier otro, sin el permiso previo por escrito de la editorial, excepto en casos de citación breve en reseñas críticas y otros usos no comerciales permitidos por la ley de derechos de autor. Para solicitar permiso, escríbale al editor a: 38-38 215 Place, Bayside, NY 11361, USA.

Work published within the framework of "Sur" Translation Support Program of the Ministry of Foreign Affairs and Worship of the Argentine Republic.

Obra editada en el marco del Programa "Sur" de Apoyo a las Traducciones del Ministerio de Relaciones Exteriores y Culto de la República Argentina.

For Gabriel, who gave my life meaning in the midst of so much pain and death.

My tribute to the deceased or disappeared
compañeras and *compañeros* who are still alive
in my memory despite the passing of time.

Beloved compañeros
dead in combat or killed by torture or betrayal
although I love a woman I do not forget you
I do not forget because I love

Juan Gelman

If history is written by the winners,
Then there must be another history.
The real history,
Like it or not...

Eduardo Mignona / Lito Nebia.

Content

Translator's Note	9
Prologue	11
Authors' Note	16
Preface	17
Part One: A Descend into Hell	19
Part Two: Thought the Cracks Comes a Light	45
Part Three: My Diary	83
Part Four: Toward Your Light, My Freedom	139
Epilogue: Reason for Writing these Memories	154
Appendix 1	158
Appendix 2	164
Appendix 3	166
Appendix 4	170

Translator's Note

This project grew out of a mutual understanding that the experiences recorded here would be beneficial to an English speaking audience. I am grateful to have had the opportunity to share and learn with María del Carmen the many ways in which language and the perception of language constantly change our understanding of the world. The challenge of finding accurate terminology for spaces that were created by the authoritarian government during this time period led me to learn about a clandestine and illegal detention system that I hope is clearly depicted by the words chosen and explained in various footnotes. Similarly, I can't begin to imagine being pregnant under these circumstances and then being separated from that child for more than 2 years, and I have tried to adhere to the meaning of the words used in the original text to transmit some of that pain. The system described here, endured by María del Carmen and the others made to disappear, might be incomprehensible to some readers in the United States because of its illegal and abusive nature, which seems a bit fantastical at times. The reality of the situation, however, is that between 200 and 500 babies were born in captivity during this time and taken away from their mothers at birth. They were given to adoptive parents, potentially with ties to the military government, while their mothers were disposed of. This is not only an illegal activity, as the commercialization of children is, but it has impacted generations of Argentinians decades after the fall of that government. The innocent but knowing voice of baby Gabriel truly illustrates the suffering that the families of those made to disappear endured and that the children of the dead mothers would endure when they found out the truth.

Gabe Salgado's work on this project has enhanced my own understanding and appreciation for the translated text and for that I am very appreciative. I am grateful to Carlos Aguasaco for his continual support of those of us who live and work in the U.S. and for promoting a more comprehensive awareness of the Hispanic experience. Some of the research for this project would not have been possible without the support from the College of Mount Saint Vincent. I am indebted to my friends and colleagues there for their support of my professional development.

I want to dedicate this translation to Mirielle Vandenheuvel for teaching me about the history of the Southern Cone and giving me the foundation to take this journey. And to the memory of Joan Lindgren, whose translation of Juan Gelman's poetry made one of the most important Spanish language poets of the 20th century accessible to an English-speaking audience. Her desire to translate this testimony planted the seed so that Gabe and I could complete the work she started and follow her legacy of inclusion and awareness.

Prologue

Remembering can be painful. Remembering can be traumatic. But having your story fall into oblivion is devastating. From 1976-1983 Argentina and her people lived through a horrific period of state terrorism. In an attempt to silence those who opposed it, the military junta exacted devastating measures that included taking control of the press, controlling the universities, and sanctioning the unlawful kidnapping and torture of thousands of citizens, and the killing and disappearing of thousands more. The objective was to silence those who opposed the regime through systemic terror and repression.

Survivors of this period have chronicled personal accounts of the brutality they or their loved ones endured, many times speaking for those who lost their voice. The nature of these testimonies can take different shapes. How survivors recall and talk about their experiences, either during and/or after their trauma impacts the listener or reader very differently. What kinds of narratives do they use? Do the details they provide follow a chronological order? What is the relationship that the survivor is seeking to establish with the listener or reader? How does one "tell" terror? The work involved in the act of remembering is difficult and traumatic, but it is necessary. It can take many shapes and be represented in many ways, but in each of its articulations, opportunities for resistance to oppression are born.

Indeed, the act of remembering and sharing those memories is in itself one of the most powerful weapons against oppression. Women's contribution to this act of recalling is key to understanding the role of memory and resistance, particularly since women's histories and stories have traditionally been silenced within cultures dominated by patriarchal norms. In her book *Dialogues of Love against the Silence. Memories of Prison, Dreams of Freedom,* María del Carmen Sillato shares a powerful account of the trauma she suffered, originally as a young disappeared woman held in an illegal and clandestine detention centre in her hometown of Rosario, and later kept as a "legal prisoner".

Sillato's memoir begins with horrific recollections of darkness, violence, and endless unknowing. Although blindfolded, she is aware that she is not alone and her first recollections bring to light the fact that she is surrounded by others who, like her, have been detained and subjected to unspeakable violence. She struggles to reconcile the human capacity for violence but somehow manages to hold on to the promise of goodness. Sillato comes to recognize the steps and voices of those around her, hears the screams of her fellow prisoners and wonders what time it might be, and when her "turn" to be interrogated might be next. As the reader delves deeper into the horror and begins to learn the names of those who suffer with her, we learn that Sillato is with child and with that revelation comes the image of light and the promise of hope that permeates the rest of the book.

Part Two of this moving memoir is titled "Through the Cracks Comes a Light" and the reader is introduced to Gabriel, Sillato's newborn son. He carries the name of the Archangel, known in many faiths as the Great Messenger, who was tasked to deliver the truth to the world and announce the promise of hope. Baby Gabriel will also serve as witness to his mother's story. He will be the voice of truth and will shed light on the darkness. Most importantly, he will break the very silence that the oppressors depend upon. Details of Gabriel's early days in at the "legal" detention centre by his mother's side fill this section of the book and offer the reader glimpses into the humanity that still manages to enter this sinister space. The kindness and support of the other women, the care of the doctor who is finally allowed in to examine Gabriel and the other newborns, and the determination to protect at all costs the new life that lives within these walls, all give new hope to the reader. Sillato creates a community with the other prisoners and shares their names with us. Time is often spent playing games of Scrabble and making crafts, and a solidarity is born. Despite their differences they are bound by their loss and by the violence they have lived. And they are also bound by the hope that the end of their nightmares is but a moment away. The daily entries in Sillato's memoir chronicle the impossible challenges of raising a young baby while in detention. Some entries are longer than others but with each one the reader feels privileged to be included in Sillato's thoughts and to bear witness to her strength. Days after turning six months of age Gabriel is given to Sillato's family, while she remains in detention. The thought of being forcibly separated from one's child is a devastation that many may try to relate to but, unless experienced, can never truly comprehend. The handing over of the child to her mother and one of her sisters is difficult to read but we too witness the scene, are strengthened by Sillato's courage and embrace Gabriel along with the arms of the author's mother and sister.

Part Three of this unique memoir, entitled "My Diary" and dedicated by Gabriel to his parents, is written by Sillato's sister Chary, who is Gabriel's guardian and, in this instance, serves as his voice. The reader is invited into a world of private letters between mother and child and Sillato's beautiful missives to her son are written poetically, speaking with hope to days ahead when they will be reunited. Gabriel's entries detail his emotional state of mind at various times and mark his growth as a young child and the important milestones he achieves. He announces his first steps to his mother, the day he first says Mamá, and details for her the family birthday parties he attends, wishing his mother were there with him throughout. The passage of time is marked by references to the changing colour of the leaves, the warmth of the summer sun, and the celebration of Christmas. Sillato's responses are filled with exclamation points, kisses, songs, tenderness, and longing. She creates word games and rhymes for her son to encourage his cooperation at bath time, and she speaks of days ahead where the two of them will walk through the parks together. With each entry the silence of the oppressor is broken and the precious bond between mother and child is nurtured and strengthened.

The book concludes with Sillato's release, and as she reunites with her son, she describes herself as moving toward the light. Several years have gone by. She has changed and her city now seems foreign to her. She feels uncertain about herself and her surroundings but her one constant is her family, and most importantly, her son, whose words gave her hope and strength throughout her darkest days. With this book Sillato exposes Argentina's dark history and offers a glimpse into the brutality lived by thousands. She names her fellow prisoners, including those whose destiny was far different from her own, and their names now live on through us. The conversation she builds with her son is touching and poignant, and notably it is powerful because it builds toward a hopeful future. This book, this dialogue of love, is indeed an act of resistance, but it is a resistance through tenderness. Indeed, *Dialogues of Love against the Silence* is a powerful and unique contribution to testimonial studies and asks that we as readers take on the role of witnesses to other witnesses and to carry on the moral duty of remembering.

We have had the privilege to experience this beautiful and intimate exchange and now we too must become messengers of hope and bear the responsibility to break the silence.

Dr. Monica Leoni
University of Waterloo
Canada

Authors' Note

This memoir was written mostly between December of 1990 and March of 1991. Ten years had to go by, however, before it was made known. In January of 2000, I sent fragments of my text and Gabriel's Diary, written by my sister Chary Sillato, to the "Memoria histórica de mujeres de Latinoamérica y el Caribe" contest and it tied for first place in the genre of testimony. Some segments of that text were published in the anthology "Redes de memoria," compiled and edited by Jorge Boccanera (Buenos Aires: Desde la gente, 2001) and "Piezas para armar nuestra memoria" (La Habana: Ediciones La memoria, 2004). They were also published in German translation by Erna Pfeiffer as "Dialoge der Liebe gegen das Schweigen" in the anthology "In Den Händen des Mondes" (Vienna: Milena Verlag, 2003).

My thanks to Nené Luchetti and Graciela Martin for their careful readings and their accurate suggestions. My thanks, also, to those who in one way or another encouraged me to publish this memoir.

M.C.S., December 2, 2005

I want to dedicate the memoirs that I wrote with so much love for and because of my nephew Gabriel to my daughter María Gracia.

Ch. S., December 2, 2005

Preface

I have been asked, and have myself wondered many times, why I haven't written about it. Why I didn't leave a testimony of those experiences. I don't know why I haven't done it yet. It could be the pain and, in particular, that terrible feeling of guilt that comes with knowing that "I lived," experienced by every survivor of genocides, that stopped my hand and the urge to write about it. I sometimes think, however, that my sons have the right to know what happened, and not through a history book—regardless of whether it depicts the true historical events. Not even through the words of other survivors. No. They have the right to learn about what happened from me because they are part of this individual history; the one that they consequently had to live. This urge might break, leaving these as just suspended words. I might also be able to break the barrier that contains them and let them fill the pages and take shape to spread this story that involves so many others.

This is a shared project. Gabriel, through the affection and voice of his Aunt Chary—María del Rosario Sillato—has contributed parts of his diary. This was written during the first year he was separated from me and it provides for a better understanding of the pain that so many children felt being forcefully separated from their parents.

This story is in a way a special homage to my mother, Agueda Cavallaro de Sillato. Her tireless fight for our freedom, her constant denunciation of our deplorable conditions, her great love and strength along each step of this painful experience have all served as and still are an inspiration in my life.

I especially acknowledge everyone who shared this road with me: my sisters Chary, Ana, Elena and Inés, whose absence would have made it very difficult to bear this grief. To my father, who is always in my thoughts; Alberto, with whom I dreamt a better world; my Aunt Josefa and my cousin Beatriz, who lit up my gray Tuesdays with their weekly visits to Devoto. To my uncle, my aunts, my nieces and nephews, my in-laws, cousins, my dear friends, and all those who appear in these pages, who tirelessly brought me strength and solace.

Lastly, these memoirs are also for my dear son Marcos, whose presence in my life kindled new fires and helped me overcome the pains of the past.

M.C.S., March 15, 1991

Note: The present narrative is based in its entirety on actual events. They might not, however, coincide with the exact dates in which they happened because of the inevitable games that the mind plays on memory, reorganizing as it deems fit the events of the past without regard for its temporal sequence. M.C.S.

Part One
A Descend into Hell

In the early hours of January 18, 1977, my partner Alberto Gómez and I, militants in the Juventud Peronista,[1] were kidnapped from the lodging where we had lived for several months in the southern area of the city of Rosario. The events of that night were completely distorted by the owner of the lodging, who said that he had seen us leave with a bag at around 11 o'clock at night accompanied by another young man who, according to his story, had come to warn us about something. This false information did not deceive my mother, who probed around the area and managed to obtain the truth from a neighbor who had witnessed everything from behind the blinds of her window. The uninterrupted search that my family carried out for almost a month was unsuccessful because our existence had been denied by the military as well as the local and federal police. Meanwhile, the story I will tell you about here began to develop at the Police Headquater's Intelligence Center, located in the heart of the city.

---

[1] This group was a political branch of the Montoneros Organization.

Dawn, January 18, 1977

A hand touches me. Touches me and brings me slowly to consciousness, I hear a voice, nearby, far away. One, two, many voices. Near? Far? In my room? I want to awaken...or do I? A hand shakes me...a voice shouts at me... and other voices, outside, now I know, are whispering...why? I don't want to wake up... is this a nightmare? Arms embrace me and I hear my name... but I don't want to wake up. Again and again. I open my eyes and what I thought was a dream looms up around me. Many voices, whispering from outside, orders, footsteps. My eyes come to rest on those of the other, the one whose voice calls me. They are immensely sad eyes, immensely bitter. Arms support me so that I can bear the truth of what is imminent, inevitable. I can feel a heart pounding... is it mine? or the heart of the one who called me by name? I am afraid, not with real fear, but with the fear one feels while watching a horror movie. This is not happening to me, this can't be real. Someone is going to suffer and I am going to be witness to this suffering. I am afraid, lest this other person not be able to pass the test. I, that other person...

...she sits up, puts her hands together and mumbles. Is she praying? "Father, take this cup from me." When the first knocks beat upon the door and the "come out with your hands up" rings throughout the room, she reaches a hand toward the other and they silently say goodbye. She then remembers the poem by Idea Vilariño that he gave her: "Cada vez cuando me voy, cada vez cuando me iba, siempre le digo hasta luego, hasta luego le decía... y nunca sé si habrá noche, ni si vuelvo a si no vuelvo."[2] The door shakes under more knocks and "come out with your hands up" sounds in her ears. She

---

[2] Each time I leave, each time I left, I always tell him see you later, see you later, I would say...and I never know if night will fall or if I will come back or not.

puts on the robe, the door opens, and she feels herself dragged and thrown against a wall. No time to think, she is nothing more than a doll sniffed out by wild beasts who also run their paws over her body and grope her.

Only one question, one, two, three times, that she answers mechanically: her name. Why so insistent? Who are they looking for? For her? She tries to comfort herself with doubt... What if it's only a routine raid? But they take her by the hair and tell her "out slowly with your hands raised high" and, once outside, she hears the sentence: "It's her," and a voice lets a name escape, not hers, not the one she told them, but the name that only her compañeros know. Her body trembles but she gives no sign. She holds herself upright, she walks without wavering. Her pride is stronger than her fear. They are taking them away, sheltered in the shadows of the night. There are many of them, some in military uniform, some in plain clothes. Does nobody see? Does nobody hear?

(I can sense frightened eyes behind the peepholes, innocent accomplices of a nighttime kidnapping, one more to add to the story of so many others.)

They force her to lie on the floor of a car, her face against the floor, she can barely breathe. From the front seat a thunderous voice assaults her. She doesn't know it yet but this is the first interrogation. They are taking her, where? to her death? No, it can't be that simple and of that she is certain. She always knew that if she was taken alive, she would have to bear her tribulations. They make her climb up on a truck, and again, face to the floor, she feels the manhandling and the sarcasm of her captors. She resists, she defends herself, and they stop. The trucks pull out and the journey starts.

Where are we going? I manage to peek out without being noticed, I want to see my city, its streets so often traveled, the trees rocking in the breeze of this summer night. I want to say goodbye... goodbye, goodbye forever. I am crying. I've suddenly awakened and I'm cold. I have awakened only to plunge myself into the midst of this nightmare.

Rectangle with Bars: Present and Future
From now until furthermore, the silence will
be minutes
From now until furthermore, the silence will
be hours
From now until furthermore will be days,
months, years
That are ripped from the calendars
Like sour fruit, ripening without sunlight

Everything is dark, cold, impassive
And that sliver of light that crashes in the corners
Seeks the heat of breathes
And the shelter of the bodies in pain
I am sure that one step away
The sad mouths that grimace with effort
Defeat the words in the end
And the wind unravels those yearnings
Where life breaks in the silence

Once, a hundred dove's beak
Cracked the brittle crystals
And the morning burst in their chest
And it was light, distance, tender breeze
Silence and light
Heat and life
Leave their damp trace
In the metal frame of the window

(It's better to wait basting mornings
In the perpendicular silences of this room
Than to mourn from day to day

The unrecognizable faces
The unrecognizable bodies punished
By the specialists in fear and pain)

Yet
I trust

I trust that the sun
That takes the shape of rectangles today
Shall melt the static lines
That crisscross the tiny window
And these wings that are tucked in arms today
Defeated travelers by exhaustion
Will fly through the infinite spaces
To where life cracks in the silence

January 18

What time can it be? I have lost all sense of time. It's been two, three, four, maybe five hours. Who knows? The blindfold keeps me from opening my eyes. I hear steps, I'm already beginning to recognize those steps. Again? I wish I could let my mind wander through memories of better times. But I can't. I feel my body drenched in sweat, a new, different sweat, with that particular smell that fear brings. I struggle to identify the nature of what I feel and I ask myself how wild animals feel when they find themselves cornered by a pack of hounds. I don't think about death, my death. From now on, perhaps, living from one moment to the next will occupy all my attention and keep me from speculating on the end of the story. They have "promised" to take me back to "la máquina"[3] when I've "cooled off a bit." I think only of this little being who has accompanied me from the very first moment. I don't know if I will

---

[3] La máquina was a common term for the electric prods used for torture.

survive, but I deeply hope that my baby will. I'm shaken by a sob. My little child, you are the only light in this darkness, you are my fortress and I will fight for us both. I hear the noise of "the machine" from the other side of the wall and my throat chokes up. They are torturing someone... is there a worse torture than to bear witness to the torture of another? And this other person, I am sure, is someone I hold tightly bound by my affection. I pray: "My God, enough, enough..."

You would like to wake up; that a hand would touch you, for a voice to call you by your name. But you know it's impossible, that you can't just slip away from the reality of a nightmare. You, the other you, look from the depths of yourself at yourself to figure out how and when this all began. But the effort exhausts you, your past and present evaporate and you slowly sink into a sleepy stupor.

When you finally wake up, you perceive the presence of another body near yours. You don't know when they could have brought it and you have no idea what time it is. You figure by the surrounding silence that it must be midnight. You look at this inert body from under the blindfold that covers your eyes and recognize it—it's your partner. First you tremble and then you feel paralyzed. You can't perceive any signs of life and you strain to detect even the slightest movement in his chest. You feel your heart might explode and still, in spite of your willing efforts, you can't speak a word. When you collect yourself, you whisper his name. There is no response and an infinite sadness overtakes you. You try again and again. After what seems like an eternity you speak in a louder voice: "If you can hear me, move your hand." You repeat this two or three times until suddenly you see his hand move slightly. You weep, knowing he is alive, in spite of the uncertain future, in spite of this endless day of torture.

January 19

Today the interrogations continued. After the questions that were accompanied by beatings and the electric prod come the formal interrogations, to be typewritten. And new beatings and formalities. And insults and manhandling, or friendliness and courtesy. If I had previously only expected harassment from them the consistency between that feeling and this reality would be less maddening than the constant uncertainty of not knowing what's going to happen next. I understand that it is part of the game, that they know perfectly well how this dichotomy wears on the mind of a prisoner, who no longer knows what to expect. The "good cop" only exists to make the cruelty of the "bad cop" seem greater by contrast. And if the same individual performs both roles, it's even worse, because, in his presence, one experiences the greatest feeling of helplessness and impotence. I find myself thinking of Mario Benedetti's *Pedro and the Captain.*

January 21

I've been brought to a room where I sense the presence of others. The footsteps of the one who brought me here have faded away beyond the doorway. I then raise my blindfold, meeting the astonished eyes that have been watching me... How young she seems, almost a child, with her blue flowered dress. She signals to me but I don't understand. Just the same, I feel enormously relieved in the presence of this other being who's awaiting my answer.

My aching body reacts to the damp floor. I shudder still at the memory of the previous night. It horrifies me to have to accept the infinite cruelty of some men. It horrifies me to know that my fate, and that of all who are here now, and who have been here and who will be here tomorrow, depends on that irrational hatred that can restrain itself from delivering a finishing blow, only so that they don't cut short the other's suffering and are able to continue enjoying the endless pain of their victims. I thought that they would finally finish me off with one blow and I almost felt relieved. I want this suffering to end, though I don't want death.

But an insistent look pulls me out of my reflections and again I meet the eyes of this child, so anxious over my silence. I smile. It's the first time I have smiled in four days and the unconscious impulse that moves my lips makes me feel strange. I smile despite the horror. I am alive. The other lips open halfway and also allow a smile to escape. "My name is Analía… Analía Urquizo, and I come from La Pampa," she murmurs. She has been shut up in this dark room for days. She fears for the fate of her boyfriend, whom the army separated her from a week ago. She fears for her brother, about whom she has been interrogated regularly. She believes in freedom, in spite of it all, and I let myself be carried along by her enthusiasm. We exchange telephone numbers and addresses to be able to notify families… in case one of us should get out first.

You think they've forgotten about you, that they won't bother you again. But they come back and take you. They say you lied and beat you again. Internally you rebel against this body of yours that is capable of bearing each blow and won't let you escape this reality by fainting. You are lucid, with an incredible lucidity that seems to allow you to understand the nature of this beating, to see yourself as the central motive for and receptacle of so much aggression.

January 22

Under the blindfold I can see only a pair of black shoes that stop before me. "How are you, kid?" The question appears ridiculous as it's obvious that I'm in a bad way, that I can hardly move. But I answer: "Last night I almost lost my baby." After a pause the voice answers: "You're going to have your baby... because you're a strong woman." How am I supposed to understand these words, spoken by one who only five days ago was carrying out the interrogation and who just yesterday made my mouth bleed with a punch? Then he adds: "La Tania was never the wife of Che Guevara, because Che was a homosexual ... The other day you asked me if I have children. Yes, I have children, and grandchildren, and I want them all to be educated according to the United States' model." When he leaves, the Pelado, a guard, approaches me: "Do you know who that was? That was the chief." The "chief," Feced, known for his irrational hatred of political activists, the chief himself had come to see me. Am I supposed to feel flattered? Ought I thank him for his "kindness"? I'm going to bear my child... what does this mean? and then what? I'm not sure yet, but perhaps these words imply a verdict of life. I'm incapable of deluding myself, I'm surrounded by death and pain, my life no longer belongs to me and I've lost all sense of the future. I live only from one moment to the next, thinking not of the outside, of freedom, but only of the possibilities that the next minute presents. Only my child distracts me from the present and carries me into the recesses of my imagination. Someone holds a child in her arms...is it me? Someone is humming a lullaby...is it me? Someone is pushing a stroller under the spring sun...is it me? My life is reduced to an interiority of fear and an outside that seems like images out of a movie. I am no more than fragments of myself, scattered about the room, sometimes laughing at the very walls, to steal from the outside world the life that at any moment may be snatched from us here.

January 24

The sound of running feet in the corridor jolts me awake. Despite the closed door I can hear the blows striking a body with incredible clarity. But what is most incredible to me is the absence of any cries of pain..."What is your name?", "Miguel..." I cannot hear the last name. As they did with me, they repeat the question over and over. And that's when I hear the voice of *la Victoria*, the famous *Polaca*, whose name was changed by the gang because she was Victor's *partner*. Hearing Victoria's rhetorical question, I feel goose bumps. "So you are the priest who married the Montoneros?" Miguel, the young Salesian priest with gentle eyes and soft voice, the one who wanted to serve God by struggling for justice on earth. My heart aches and I'm overcome with sobbing. It must be two or three in the morning. Something serious is happening because they have stopped harassing Miguel. I hear whispering among the guards...it seems that they've brought someone else, who seems to be seriously injured, perhaps already dead. The whole place fills with a deadly silence.

10:30 in the morning

I ask the guard to take me to the bathroom. I want to see Miguel and perhaps the other one, the wounded *compañero*. This time I openly spy in front of the guard, but he does nothing to stop me, as if he didn't care. And he doesn't, because there is nothing new or interesting to see. As it turns out, the corridor is deserted and the doors to the interrogation and torture rooms are both open. There is no one there, and no sign of anything that could help me find out what happened last night. I must have been asleep when they took them out of here. They must have done it secretly, in silence. Will I ever hear of them again?

January 25

Today, Pelado[4] allowed me to go into the basement to shower. There, I have met some new faces, those that belong to the voices that reach me in this tiny room into which each day more people are brought. Someone, a small woman with a smile on her lips and the saddest eyes gave me a towel, a shirt, and a pair of jeans. Her warmth and tenderness have profoundly touched me. We didn't share a word but I felt a great compassion for my suffering in that gesture. We are a handful of lonely souls, joined by the same pain.

January 26

Last night this sinister place was again filled with shouting, running, and crying. They have "worked" all night trying to wring words out of the newly arrived. It's said that they belong to the Poder Obrero.[5] The incredibly loud volume of the radio has not been enough to cover over such suffering. I felt the hands of Analía searching for mine and squeezing them so as to join her fear and pain with mine and give us the strength to endure this horror.

This morning they have dragged the body of a young man to this room. Two hours later the guard came in furious: someone had gotten away from them. I mentally enjoy the situation, thinking of the fate of the one who escaped and praying that they don't find him. But at the same time I am shaken by the hatred and fury that this incident has unleashed in these men. I hear the beatings and questions to the other *compañeros,* and the screams of pain fuse with the screams of rage. They have come into this room, handcuffed the young

---

[4] Nickname for one of the members of the police gang
[5] The "Organización Comunista Poder Obrero," was a militant political organization that was harshly repressed under the dictatorship.

man, "so that you don't also get away from us," and hit him hard on the head for good measure. Now that the others have left, I look at him from below my blindfold. He is shaking, sobbing and afraid. I suddenly feel an infinite tenderness for this overgrown boy who has now entered the irreversible condition of "the disappeared," a condition that unites us and turns us into links in a chain that was begun almost a year ago and is not yet finished. I would like to ask him his name, tell him that I understand his pain, that it is the same as mine, to transmit that faith that at every moment I fight to keep alive. But we cannot talk, a "curfew" has been imposed and any whisper can awaken suspicion. I can feel them spying on us, trying to catch us in the middle of some forbidden conversation. They don't realize that we are also learning to perceive them, that the blindfolds are less of an impediment to recognizing them and distinguishing them from us with each passing day. We now know when they are watching us and when we have some respite, when the more relentless guard is on and when it's the "lenient" one, when it's time for torture and when it's time for rest, when they have obtained some information and when they have not obtained anything. We can recognize their good and bad moods, and are cheered up by their "bad mood" and saddened by their "good mood." We know that they have not found Lito, that the hunt has been fruitless, and that this has them troubled, uneasy, and angry. They take turns blaming each other for the oversight. They take their anger out on the prisoners every so often so as not to be overwhelmed by it.

Before I have a chance to speak with the handcuffed *compañero,* they come and take him away. Soon after, spirits begin to calm and we slowly return to the "normal" routine. It's nighttime and each person sinks into their own thoughts, trying to escape the heavy silence that surrounds us.

January 27
"LT8, Rosario Radio station brings you the news at eight o'clock."

Rosario: At midnight today, during a raid the provincial police conducted on a house located in this city, five subversives were brought down, three women and two men. They resisted police orders, leading to a confrontation that also resulted in the wounding of an officer from Precinct 18. The subversives were militants of the Poder Obrero. This information was obtained through materials belonging to this left-wing terrorist organization that were seized by the police. Among the seized objects was a printer, which would indicate that the house was used by the aforementioned terrorist group as a center for the printing of subversive material. Furthermore…"

They turned off the radio abruptly, but it's too late, the news has reached every single prisoner. The place is filled with electrical appliances: a refrigerator, a washing machine ("Pelado, do you want this washing machine?". "No man, not interested, it's missing the top cover. Besides, I already took one"), a fan, and also a small printer (Fragile/Made in Italy) still in the box used to ship it by airmail. Last night they took away the prisoners who had been kidnapped two days ago, everyone except Lito who had escaped earlier. Two women and three men, and it is said that they were members of Poder Obrero.

January 27 (in the afternoon)
You have been told to get ready, that the "military judge" will be coming today. You don't understand much about these internal formalities and procedures, but you're suspicious. That is the only feeling you have

learned in your brief experience as a prisoner. You are not the only one being interviewed; they have also brought a young woman from the basement. You've heard that those in the basement are a bit closer to a life sentence than a death sentence. She sits on the floor next to you and you watch her. She is very nervous and she can't stop moving one of her legs. You watch her again, and then you're bathed in cold sweat: it's her, and only a month ago you were mourning her passing. No, it's not an error, that is what they said on the outside, perhaps to stop any attempts to search for her. It's her and she is alive. You whisper to her: "Marisol," and she is startled. You soothe her: "It's me, Inés' sister. Don't worry, no one knows we know each other." Marisol, my sister's classmate, the one who so many times brought us to tears laughing with her quirky behavior, the one who had overcome distance and silence while waiting with admirable patience for her partner's return from a prison in Rawson during the previous dictatorship.[6] She knows from what she was told in the morning that it is almost certain that her fate will be decided today. You can feel the anguish and uncertainty in the grimace of her mouth...How do you give her hope if you don't have any?... They come for you. You have the "honor" of being the first and, therefore, you don't know what is waiting for you, but you can sense it because they take you to the torture chamber...

I want these tribulations to end... For the first time I truly feel that my peace and rest could only be possible with my death. And I ask, I beg Darío, the "good one" of the gang, to rest his revolver on my temple and shoot... I saw all of their faces when my blindfold fell during one of the electric prodding sessions...I have seen their

---

[6] The previous military dictatorship took place in Argentina between 1966 - 1973. Many political militants were killed or imprisoned. With the return to democracy in 1973, all political prisoners were pardoned and freed.

emotionless faces and their concentration as they tried to do "their jobs" perfectly. Ciego[7] and the "military judge" were there showing, perhaps, that the *picana*[8] applied to the head, the mouth, the neck, and the breasts, with the help of another *picana* applied at the same time to the belly and legs, knowing as they do about my pregnancy, was an efficient way to destroy the prisoner's body and morale. Monsters, monsters, and among them, Nacho, that childhood neighbor with whom I had occasionally shared some fun and outings... Nacho... how could I imagine him in this "job" behind his formal and polite facade?

When they bring you back to the room, Marisol and Analia are still there. They help you sit on the floor with them and squeeze your hands to contain your trembling. Marisol wets her fingers with the tea and moistens your dry lips. You cry for your son, for you and for everyone, for the irreparable damage that they are inflicting on the prisoners. You hear Marisol's voice say: "Don't be afraid, your son will be born healthy and beautiful, don't let them destroy your hope," and you feel that little by little you reconcile with your faith. Those images and the reality that surrounds you fade away under the blindfolds as you drift into unconsciousness.

A commanding voice returns me to the present: "María Sol Pérez-Losada, Analía Urquizo, you are being transferred." Several hours must have passed since I lost consciousness. The silence indicates that it's midnight. I try to understand what is happening, I don't know if the "military judge" has interviewed them already, I don't know where they are being transferred at this hour. There is no time to talk, only for a long hug and

---

[7] Ciego was the nickname of the torturer José Rubén Lofiego, an expert in applying the electric prod.
[8] The picana is a wand or prod that delivers a high voltage but low current electric shock to a victim being tortured.

wishes of good luck. When they take them away, I lay on the floor and begin to shake violently, indicating that my mind has read between the lines and understood the hidden message in that "harmless" order. Darío brings me a blanket and lifts my blindfold. Our eyes meet and my question no longer makes sense: "Where are they taking them?" I know the answer and he knows it, so he shakes his head and says: "Stay calm. Nothing is going to happen to you."

January 30

My entire body hurts. My left knee was dislocated during the last interrogation and a big bruise is starting to cover the back of my leg. The pain has been unbearable. When they were taking me back to the room, someone stopped behind me and asked: "Do you know who I am?" It was Nacho, but I said that I didn't know him. Then he said: "You idiot, look what you got yourself into!"

I also have another problem with my left arm. About three days ago I found the spring of a pen on the floor of the room. Since there is nothing to do, I figured I would stretch it out and make it into a nice bracelet. I remember when they took me to see the "military judge" he asked me what that was and I told him it was nothing, just the spring of a pen. Something silly one does without thinking of the consequences. The fact is that that tiny piece of metal served as a magnified conductor of electricity. The arm has swollen incredibly and I have lost feeling in my hand. Pollo[9], in an act of solidarity, brought me a wet towel to lower the inflammation. This was immediately followed by Jorge janking the towel away while yelling: "Who was stupid enough to put

---

[9] Pollo was the nickname of a kidnapped militant who by then was collaborating with the police.

that wet towel on her?" Later I learned that the moisture could have killed me by coming into contact with my electrified body. Life is a constant source of learning and even in that unfortunate horrific experience I have come away with new knowledge.

February 1

This morning they brought two young women to this room. They were not blindfolded and both were terribly afraid. The reason: they had been caught at a motel or a park. I couldn't really understand what they were saying to each other, but their only worry was their parents' reaction when they found out. The two young men who were brought in with them were being questioned in the office next door. They were all from the nearby town of Santa Fe and they had come to Rosario to have some fun. That fun was going to cost them! They have been taken away now; I want to believe that they were let go because I haven't heard anything to the contrary. The amazing thing is that those girls saw me lying there, blindfolded, and, worried as they were about their own futures, never attempted to connect in any way with me. Hopefully they were let go because it seemed to me that they were not even aware of the country in which they lived. If they did leave, they took away my only chance of sending a message to my family with them.

February 2

I am here alone. There is a small set of stairs leading to a mezzanine that was built in a rush to house some of the kidnapped. *The compañeros,* with a bit of humor to break the tension from the fear, have named the place "la fabela," referring to the misery that characterized the Brazilian shanty towns. My partner and two more *compañeros* are there. My friend Zapato was taken away with Analía and Marisol. Pelado came by this afternoon and made them come down so that Pollo could mop the place. For the first time in days, randomly, or at the order of Pelado, I have been allowed this brief encounter with my partner. We have placed ourselves next to each other surreptitiously. His arm touched mine and we shared a few words while staring into each other's eyes with our blindfolds slightly lifted. He suddenly leaned over and kissed me on the lips, and that show of affection, that caress in the face of such horror, has broken the thread that linked me to reality and has caused me to faint.

I smile now remembering the incident. I had begged many times during the beatings that I would pass out, so that a curtain could fall on the drama being performed. I never had any luck, not even when Gatica,[10] in one of his hateful fits, banged my head against the wall and I slid to the floor, dazed and bewildered.

Today I learned another truth: our bodies react to and resist external aggressions with the same strength as they can respond to a caress. The brusque contrast, the unforeseen passage from one state of mind to another, has greatly impacted me and I have needed a few seconds of unconsciousness to assimilate the new message. I reflect: love is stronger than hate and it has allowed me to escape for a moment from the painful awareness of this reality.

February 3 at dawn

They promise you that they will take you to the basement if you tell them what illegal activities your sisters are involved in. The basement for you is a real bridge that would distance you from this room in which you have been lying for more than fifteen days,

---

[10] Nickname of a member of the police gang.

permanently waiting for new sessions of torture and harassment. That is why you take the deal, knowing that the only thing you could tell them will be the story of your family's pain over your disappearance. And that is what you do. They return once and again to the same point, hoping that you will finally prove their suspicion that your sisters—one or all of them, it doesn't matter— are involved in something illegal. These were baseless suspicions but necessary for obtaining more information that would allow them to return to the excitement of the hunt. There are many of them and their questions are ridiculous: "What if we go to your house now and your sisters are 'up'?[11] You take his words and answer calmly: "Yes, up and around at two in the morning trying to console my mother who is distraught over my absence." They threaten you, they yell at you, but they already know that you will stand by your answers until the end and they will miss out on the chance of other kidnappings. They could do it anyway if they want because the act itself would restore their self confidence and the authority that the military has bequeath them. We have been in this same round of senseless questioning for over an hour. They get bored, tired and finally stop the interrogation and take you back to the room. You duck your head trying to hide the triumphant smile that you are afraid has escaped your lips. You are glad that the blindfold hides the twinkle of excitement and victory in your eyes. You, who are like a tiny insect trapped in a spiderweb. You have won another battle and cannot stop the feeling of satisfaction and joy that this has produced.

February 3
"Sir, I must be informed of my husband's whereabouts. I need to speak to my lawyer." I, returning from

---

[11] "Up" here means "ran away."

my dream, am confused by the words "informed" and "lawyer," two legal terms in such an illegal place. I would laugh out loud if not for the anguish I perceive in this new voice, which I imagine has just been brought to this room. I have been alone since they took Marisol, Analía and Zapato and the idea of having someone close by to share these endless hours makes me feel good, though I feel a bit selfish for the human cost it entails. When the guard leaves, I lean my head and watch her under the blindfold: I see a person in her late 40s. She is immobile, as if a cataclysm has paralyzed her will to move. There is no way to make contact with her. She is lying on the floor in the opposite corner of the room. If I raise my voice to talk to her, I could be heard and they would immediately come into the room.

The promise to take me down to the basement after that nocturnal interrogation has not been kept yet. In any case, I am not hopeful that it would be kept, that would not be consistent with their contradictory behavior. Besides, logic dictates that if they didn't get what they wanted from me they didn't have to keep their promise either. However, every time Managua[12] stops by the room, I ask him: "When are you taking me down there?" and every time he says: "Are you sure you want to go down there instead of out to freedom?" and I say: "Yes, I am sure." Now that Managua has stopped circulating around, I lie down and watch my companion of misfortune without her noticing. She has lifted her blindfold a bit and looks at me with such bewilderment and surprise that it makes me instantly understand that she has no idea about this place or the situation she is in. She probably thinks that the offer of freedom was sincere and that I said no either because I am afraid to leave this place or because I have completely lost my mind.

---

[12] Nickname for a member of the police gang.

Her naiveté no longer amuses me; rather, it makes me profoundly distressed to think about all of the people on the outside who have preemptively blindfolded themselves so as not to have to learn about the horrors of this reality. I know that it will only take a few hours for her to see that she has been invited to be part of this game of cat and mouse, but for now she still believes in justice and deserves my respect.

February 5

"Take these two down to the basement!" I recognize *Carlitos'* voice and start thinking that the command might be real. My heart is a swirl of emotions but I react instantly: "And what would the fate be of those in the "fabela"? I am wondering what is going to happen to my partner. Then, I hear *Carlitos'* footsteps climbing the stairs. After a moment, he says: "And take these down also." The command doesn't mean the end of these tribulations, nor the beginning of a better chapter. Even so, this doesn't stop us from being overrun with happiness and hope.

February 6

Nelly has been taken to the basement along with me. The two days that she spent lying on the floor blindfolded, asking about her husband, asking to speak to a lawyer, and only getting laughter or indifference in response from the guards, have made her acutely aware of a reality that less than 72 hours ago she could not have even imagined existed. However, there is no resentment, just an intimate understanding of our suffering. Because of this, an honest friendship has rapidly sprung up between us. She takes care of me like an older sister, making sure that I eat, that I am not startled, that I take care of myself given the state I am in. She embraces me with a protective gesture. She has been reunited with her husband here. They have not been detained for political reasons but as payback from some police chief since the husband is a lawyer.

I have also met Stellita and her boyfriend in this basement. They are both very young. I have also been able to become friends with her easily. There are more men here, only us three women. The woman who had passed me the jeans and shirt is no longer here. The guards are patrolling, they give us the "honor" of a visit from time to time while treating us with a disconcerting familiarity. Jorge, who only a few days ago had hit me in the stomach with the butt of his rifle and another time kicked me while accusing me of watching him from under my blindfold, is now concerned about my pregnancy. Managua stops by often during his shifts and tells us that he has three children, two biological and one "adapted."[13] Perhaps their change in attitude that began once we were moved to the basement indicates a change in their perspective of the prisoners: before we were nothing more than objects, if that. Now, we have names and the uncertain promise of becoming legalized, which is to say that we are regaining our humanity. We are not, however, allowed to leave the room or speak with the other *compañeros*. This is something we do when they are back upstairs and busy.

February 8

You tell me that you don't know what is going to happen to you; that you might not survive. So you take off your ring and give it to me: "This way I can always be close to you, regardless of what happens," you whisper. I tell you about my fears and our baby. You ask me to pick a name. If he is a boy, Gabriel, I say firmly. Gabriel was the name that you gave him when he was only

---

[13] He mistakes "adopted" with "adapted."

beginning to be a presence for us. And if she is a girl, her name will be Lucía. Lucía, light, warmth, sun, hope. I know the baby is still alive because I felt movement inside me today and, for a moment, I allowed myself to be filled with joy and confidence. But new fears and anguishes have leaked in through crevices. I don't know what kind of damage the torture might have caused the baby. You ask me to have faith, to not abandon this fight for life because I carry within me a sun that drives away the present shadows. I lay my head on your shoulder and tell you how much I miss having your arms around my waist at night. I feel your hand caressing my hair and I close my eyes to forget this damp basement for a moment; to forget the peeling walls, the miniscule barred openings high above us at street level, through which hardly any sunlight enters. Your warmth shelters and protects me. I would like to prolong this moment forever but I know the "illegal" nature of this encounter and the dangerous consequences if we are discovered. This is why I tell you that I am always thinking of you and that you are always with me. I kiss you and move away sadly. Your arms are now empty of me and the pain becomes water in your eyes. I fight away the thought that this might be the last time I see you. It's possible you might be thinking the same thing. I run to my room/cell and I collapse on the mat that serves as a bed and all of my feelings of rage and impotence explodes in an inconsolable cry.

February 9

I observe the line formed by the *compañeros* from a safe distance. Each one of them has a small improvised bag of clothes that, like the ones I am wearing, probably belonged to others whose fates only God knows. They were told last night that they would be taken to the jail in Coronda. An air of uncertainty and distrust invades the place. Everyone knows that the same announcement has led many to their deaths. Accusations of attempted escape were an easy excuse, already used on other occasions. I anxiously try to find my partner's eyes but I think he finds it difficult to lift his head and meet mine. How do we say goodbye, goodbye forever? The line starts to move, and then he turns his head and we take a long look at each other. He tries to smile but it turns into a painful grimace. He lifts his hand to his lips and sends me a kiss. That kiss restores my faith. "See you tomorrow," I whisper, "see you tomorrow" because there will be a tomorrow; I am sure of it. "I love you," I tell him, I tell myself, as I bring my hands to my lips and send him a kiss.

Part Two
Thought the Cracks Comes a Light

Monday, July 11, 1977. 11:50 p.m.
An intense pain bursts in my womb at the same time that a jailer and an armed guard drag me through the unending hallway. My hands are cuffed under my belly and I take deep breaths. I feel a rush of emotions: fear, anxiety, joy, impatience. A miracle is about to happen, the first one in many months: the miracle of life over death. They take my handcuffs off and I lie on the stretcher. A woman, an angel in my eyes, gets closer and caresses my head: "Everything will be fine," she tells me, and she pronounces my name with tenderness. I compare my physical pain now with that of a few months ago, and that gives me the strength to cope with it. That was senseless suffering, born of hatred and cruelty. This is just a step towards the light, a light that is already slipping through my legs; pulling with it an infinite sense of peace. I hear crying. I laugh and cry, and this room lights up as if a tiny firefly has vanquished the shadows. Today I pick up the pieces of myself once more, in you and for you, my son. Today I am once more able to fly, tied to the light of your comet.

Gabriel
Son, I say
Son who lays your head on my heart
To cradle my sleep
To fill my life
Son, I say
So that your tenderness never fades
So that you survive this pain
So that you conquer fear
Son, who has fought death

And has made joy sprout
In the damp corners of the sorrow
Open your eyes and see

You are a witness to this history
The true history
And I name you
Gabriel

Gabriel
So that you announce the truth
Gabriel
So that you announce the life
Gabriel
So that you defeats the silence

Early morning of Tuesday, July 12

I open my eyes. The light of the streetlamps shines in through the windows, allowing me to see my surroundings. I have been handcuffed to the bed, as if I had the strength to make a run for it in my present state. I don't feel sorry for myself, I no longer care about anything else because I can reach out with my free hand and stroke the small damp head and warm body in the crib they have placed by my side. I am ashamed by the pain my mother feels seeing me like this. Major Soria has granted her permission to spend the night by my side. It hasn't been easy, but her patience and powers of persuasion have basically wrested this concession from him. Now she is here and she has fallen asleep with her head resting on my bed. I understand the confusion that must be playing out in her head, the joy for a new birth and the sorrow for the uncertain future. I heard her ask Colorada[14] to uncuff me and it broke my heart. I

---

[14] Nickname of one of the female wardens.

tried to calm her, saying that nothing could threaten the happiness of these moments. We then both fell asleep, her hand stroking my head and my hand searching for the warmth of my son.

Tuesday, July 12 at 6 a.m.
Colorada is off duty and another guard, Carmen, has just arrived to replace her. I know Carmen well. She is very much a police officer, but up until now I had not realized her ability to evaluate situations wisely. As soon as she saw me handcuffed to the bed she made my mother leave the room and, for the first time, I had the pleasure of seeing Colorada humiliated by her superior. To my surprise, she ordered that my handcuffs be taken off immediately and that from that moment on my family could be in the room with me with the door closed and that the guard, whoever she was, would stay outside. Then she made a most appropriate comment: "Because what are we to the military? Nothing! And you think that we can overlook their orders!" Good for Carmen, she put Colorada in her place and made her own place clear. She brought my mother back into the room and, shutting the door behind her, left us alone.

July 12
Chary and Ana have spent the day with me in shifts. The orders are that only one is allowed in at a time. My mother will be back tonight. Elena and Inés will come by later and they might bring Cecilia and Daniela. I feel so many emotions that I forget my current situation for a moment.

Olga is, in part, responsible for this happiness. She was the one who defied Elsa's, the head warden, orders not to notify my family—which was actually contrary to the commander's orders. During one of my mother's visits, Olga told her that I was in labor. Chary started roaming around the Asistencia Pública[15] and Olga was punished without visitors for a month. At 10:45 in the evening, when they had given up on the possibility that I would be taken to the Asistencia that night and Chary had already gone home, the phone rang. A doctor who had found out about my possible arrival from Chary called to tell her that I was already there. It was an anonymous but friendly voice. The wardens were so angry when my mother and Ana arrived half an hour later that they strip searched them. I didn't learn of the great humiliation they suffered until much later because they didn't want to cloud the happiness we were feeling.

Gabriel sleeps, he has slept the whole time. Perhaps he is dreaming of being in my womb, perhaps he is trying to delay his inevitable encounter with this world and its cruel reality. Don't be afraid, my son. Together we will plant flowers there, where they say that grass will never grow again.

July 13
Despite the doctor's promise to keep me in the Asistencia Pública for 48 hours, an order has arrived calling for me to be returned to the Alcaidía this morning, without delay.[16] I get up listlessly, I still feel weak. My sisters Elena and Inés—who had come to visit me with my dear Cecilita—wait behind the door, trying to contain the anguish and disappointment that inundates them.

I now retrace my steps. I roam the same hallways as two nights ago, escorted once more by the jailers and two guards, rifle in hand. But now Elena, Cecilita, and

---

[15] Community clinic.
[16] The Alcaidía is a prison unit located inside a police headquarters and was used to hold minor offenders and those awaiting trial. During the dictatorship, they were used to house and torture female political prisoners until their transfer to larger prisons.

Inés walk elbow-to-elbow with me, forming a protective wall around me. In a few more steps we will part ways, but I will cherish the brief and intense intermission that reuniting with my family brought me. Elena carries Gabriel in her arms with such tenderness that the tension of the moment is dispelled. Inés is quiet but her eyes glisten with emotion and sadness. Cecilia is in her arms, happy with her new cousin, oblivious to the pain that surrounds us. I walk with my head held high before the curious stares of the onlookers, defying any signs of compassion I may find on their faces. My son has been born alive and healthy. Is this not the greatest gift life has given me?

Elena hands Gabriel back to me at the door to the clinic. We hug but our voices refuse to utter a goodbye. When the police car takes off I look at Gabriel. His eyes, now open, look up to meet mine. I hug him to my chest and close my eyes. I don't want him to see me cry...

July 13, at noon

The door to the prisoners' wing[17] opens and a stream of familiar faces, my *compañeras,* lets a smile slip across the few meters that still separate us and sweeps across my face and soul. A happy murmur hangs in the air. Countless arms hug me, give me courage, make my return less difficult. There is Tere with Eduardito, Nené with Cristina, and "Cangu" with Juan Marcelo. It's a tribute to a new birth, the fourth in the last six months. I hug Lala and we cry together, for the little brother of hers who could not be and for his mother who chose to accompany him on his journey to the other side. This is also my family. The dampness of this basement gives way before the warmth of this home.

---

[17] These spaces, referred to as "pabellones" in Argentina, were big rooms used as overflow housing for prisoners. From here on they will be translated as "wings."

July 22

Today, for the first time in so many months, a pediatrician has come, sent by the Command to see the boy born a little over a week ago. He asked to see Gabriel. Apparently everything was in order. Before leaving to the infirmary I want to make sure that the doctor will see the other children, and I ask him to do so. He looks at me perplexed and then turns to the nurse and the jailer. "Are there more children here?" The jailer responds by lowering her eyes and nodding affirmatively. I explain that we are worried about Juan Marcelo, who is now a month old and is very small and cries all the time. The doctor says: "I want to see them all."

Eduardito and Cristina are well. Juan Marcelo, on the other hand, is an incredible example of the tenacity of life. Dealt yet another bad hand by destiny, his mother does not have enough milk to feed him and the lack of medical attention has made things worse. The pediatrician has ordered an emergency feeding regimen to treat his rickets. The sweet privilege of feeding him has fallen to me. He is now fastened to my chest and I feel the force of his little mouth extracting my milk and satiating an ancient hunger. "Cangu" is at my side and we look at one another. No words are spoken, only a smile and a quiet complicity... from mother to mother...

Early morning of July 29

It was only nine in the evening but I had been overcome by exhaustion and fell into a deep sleep. For this reason I struggled to return to reality and understand what was happening. I sat up in my bed and just in that moment I realized that the lights were on and the jailer was saying my name and telling me to follow her to her office. I remembered that that afternoon I had asked for a doctor to see Gabriel about an allergic reaction, and

I asked the jailer if I should bring my son. I noticed a tremor in her voice when she said no, and a chill ran through my body. I also saw the fear in the eyes of my *compañeras* and determined that it was about two in the morning. I looked at Gabriel, who slept by my side, and got up silently. My movements were awkward, as if my body didn't recognize my mind's commands. When I entered the office the three men waiting there turned to look at me. Then one of them said: "We are going to ask you some questions and you better answer truthfully. If you don't, you already know, we'll take you back there again." His voice made me tremble, a sinister, "familiar" voice. I looked at his face and recognized him, it was "el Ciego," a master of the art of the electric prod. I tried to stay calm. They brought names and photos. I must respond firmly, without giving any signs that would allow them to discover that I was lying to them. I noticed doubt and confusion among them. Their doubt was heartening to me. Finally, they let me return to the wing, but promised that they would be back. Again, "el Ciego" yelled to me: "if you lied to us, you better prepare yourself because you know what's in store for you."

When I was back in the wing I stumbled across la Negra, who they had also called over for interrogation. Our gazes met, I tried to warn her with my eyes about what was awaiting her, and she thanked me with a knowing wink. Soon after she returned with the same fear in her eyes and the same threat hanging over her head.

Our *compañeras* silently surrounded us. Some took our hands in theirs, others gave us hugs. My body felt frigid and my teeth were chattering. We now remembered the magnitude of the danger we were still in. The Intelligence Center was only a few meters away, that secret detention center that was within the police headquarters, the place in which every one of this small group of survivors had played chess with death... the place where no doubt others—the owners of the names we were asked about or the faces in the photos—were playing their turns.

July 29
As if sent by a guardian angel, my mom and Aunt Horacia came to visit me this morning. I told them about the events of last night and no doubt the fear in my voice led them to interrupt their visit and go see the Commander to request an explanation. A while later they returned with a new visitation permit and a message from Major Soria: my *compañeras* and I should know that we will not be taken from this jail, that we are all under his jurisdiction and nothing would be done without his permission. The irony! We are being protected by none other than an officer of the infamous Argentine army. We laughed, some of us at the absurdity of this apparent contradiction, and others, perhaps, clinging to that same absurdity so as to feel a bit safer. We will see if this assurance is kept.

July 31
I haven't had milk to feed Gabriel for the last two days. The terrifying events of the other night dried up my breast milk and not even Major Soria's "reassurance order" has been able to put me at ease. So I have decided to heat up some milk and try to bottle feed him. But I am distracted and attentive to any sound of the locking and unlocking of the wing's doors. I am so absentminded that when I can't turn off the hotplate, I hurry to get a wet towel to put out the flames and, in doing so, I glaze the red-hot coils with the fingertips of my left hand. The pain is absolutely unbearable and I am unable to take my hand out of a bucket of cold water without feeling

the jabbing pain and the pulsing of all five fingers. Maybe my fingerprints will be erased for now since they have almost completely disappeared and the swelling has reached my fingernails. A nurse has stopped by and has given me a cream but I am still unable to take my hand out of the cold water. And my poor Gabriel! He is now without breast milk and without a mother who can change his diapers and carry him in her arms. But, what are aunts for? Aunt Piqui has happily taken over the role of substitute mother and Gabriel, who already knows her well because he sleeps between us in a double bed, doesn't mind her taking over.

August 5

Our fears were not unfounded. Despite Major Soria's presumptuous assurances, I was taken to be interrogated again last night. I sense that someone at the Intelligence Center has mentioned my name and they are trying to connect the dots. Their attitude is different this time, which leads me to believe that the pressure that my mother and aunt are putting on the lead commander is making something of a difference. I am unsettled by the "kindness" of the torturers who address me as if they were asking for permission. If I held strong last time even while being threatened, why should I loosen up now? They left without answers once again, but this time there were no threats.

August 9

There are four babies in this big family: Cristinita was the first one to arrive. Even though she was due at the beginning of January, she refused to come into this world until almost two weeks later. Nené, her mother, and her dear grandmother Juani (that woman who had given me the jeans and shirt at the Intelligence Center) have been through a lot of pain. When the police and gang had raided her parents' home, Cristinita had lost her father, her aunt, and two of their friends. In other words, Juani lost two of her children on the same day, and the third one, Guillermo Juan, has been missing for several months. The other two children in our big family, Eduardito and Juan Marcelo, belong to two sisters: Tere and Gladis. They were brought to the Alcaidía together with another sister, Tita, the oldest who was also pregnant and had a 19-year-old daughter, Lala. They were particularly cruel with Lala at the Intellingent Center, I imagine to punish her mother because they didn't have the nerve the torture a woman who was eight months pregnant. Since no medical attention had been given, Tita didn't know that her pregnancy had ended a few days earlier. When she found out it was too late and she died during surgery. Eduardo was born on March 25, Juan Marcelo on June 15, and finally Gabriel arrived. We have asked to be let out to the yard at least once a day for the sake of the babies, but this request has not been granted yet (and it might never be). We have all worked to make this place as cozy as possible for the babies, damp and gray as it is, which is why the smokers now go to a room in the back of the wing so that they don't pollute the air.

We share a certain religious formation, let's call it Catholic, Apostolic and Roman. Some of us are more practicing than others, some more distanced from the church than others, and some are more indifferent than others. Someone, however, has suggested that we baptize the babies and most of us have agreed. So today we are having a party to celebrate. Juani is in charge of baptizing them and Piqui has agreed to be Gabriel's godmother. Even though this is mostly a symbolic act, we have used it to express our desire to build bonds and relationships with each other that will endure beyond the circumstances that led us to meet under this roof.

August 15

My sisters have used their powers of persuasion during their last visit to convince me that Gabriel and his father should meet. We would be separated for only two or three days. Chary and Mom will travel to the Coronda jail and uncle Moncho will go in to visit his brother with Gabriel. It will be a surprise for Alberto. Though it hurts me to be separated from my little lion cub I understand the reasons and I agree to the plan. Chary is working on getting us a marriage license from the Commander because without it my family would not be able to visit Alberto. I anxiously await the call to hand Gabriel over to my sister. I hope that my little one doesn't miss me as much as I will miss him. The jailer comes, takes Gabriel in her arms, and leaves. This is just a temporary separation... What am I going to do when he turns 6 months old?[18]

August 16

Time slows down without Gabriel around. I feel a physical and emotional emptiness, and nothing can make me feel better. Hilda finds me to play a game of scrabble, a game she and I have enjoyed playing and arguing over, since I am pretty sure she cheats with some of the words. But there is great complicity between us. I will never forget the great risk she took a few days after I had first been taken to the Alcaidía. During a visit with her mother they exchanged handkerchiefs and she whispered that there was a phone number written on that handkerchief. And then she asked her to call my family and let them know I was there. And that sweet woman did so and because of her my family learned of

---

[18] The military allowed the babies born in captivity to be with their mothers for the first 6 months.

my whereabouts. Hilda is older than I am. Her children are in their twenties and they have taken her hostage so that one of her sons would surrender. She doesn't complain because she would rather be the one in here instead of him. She fears that she will suffer the same fate as Blanca, who had also been taken as a hostage only to learn much later that her son was killed at the exact moment she was taken. Or the same thing that happened to Herminia, who just found out that her daughter has been killed in a skirmish. There are so many painful stories here that I feel selfish thinking only about my absent Gabriel. So I put on my best smile and start a game of scrabble with Hilda.

August 18

I have a visitor. I go out and my mother is waiting for me, along with Ana and Gabriel. I run to them and hug them and tighten my arms around my baby. He seems bigger, more mature after his adventure away from Mom. They tell me that Alberto had the biggest surprise of his life, that his first reaction was to ask "what is this kid doing here?" and that, filled with emotion, he took him in his arms and did not stop hugging and caressing him the entire time. For those of us who have been deprived of so many basic things, each experience, each moment brings endless emotions. Our separation, my son, was worth it because your father's resolve has been strengthened by the warmth of your presence.

August 20

That my Aunts Horacia and María are nuns of the order of the Good Shepherd and my Uncle Sebastián is a brother with the Redentorists must play in my favor with the Commander. I know the long arm of the military terror has reached many representatives of Christ on this earth, but for some reason my family's religiosity—whether it is my uncle's constantly petitioning the Commander for my release or my Aunt Horacia always accompanying my mother when she goes to make inquiries, has translated into small gains that have benefited all of us who share the basement space of the Alcaidía. Nothing has been done without endless trips and long waits at the Command Office, but their persistence has paid off. The benefit of better nutrition for nursing and expecting mothers was granted a few days before Juan Marcelo was born. This has unleashed a network of solidarity among the family members and neighbors who stop by to bring us small presents. We celebrate the arrival of food on Wednesdays. The guards complain that the three authorized families bring so much food. We know about the solidarity, the meetings in the street corners so that all the other families can contribute to the basket. Juani is getting ready to peel the potatoes to make gnocchis for everyone while Liliana tastes the half of one of the avocados that my neighbor, María Elena, sends weekly. Afterwards she uses the skin to make an elaborate facial mask. Wednesdays are our break day and, if we are in a good mood, we put on a small play. Right now we are rehearsing *The Importance of Being Earnest* by *Oscar Wilde.*

Speaking of benefits, my family got permission to baptize Gabriel today (one more baptism!) at the police station itself, taking advantage that Moncho, Alberto's brother, will be in Rosario for a couple of more days before returning to Corrientes. Moncho is the godfather and Inés the godmother. The ceremony was modest but very emotional, given the circumstances. Afterwards, my family left behind a tray of pastries to share with the *compañeras.* The jailers, of course, kept the best pieces for themselves.

August 20

Since my arrival at the Alcaidía, my artistic specialty has been making engravings on bones. Liliana first taught me how to do it, and since then I have spent hours working on it every day as my prison labor. It keeps me entertained and I take joy in my finished works. The key is to rescue the snail bones that don't have grease stains and always keep a well-sharpened hairpin. To sharpen it, we scrape it against the base of the sink that is in the kitchen. I have taken up this work again today since my fingertips are healing. I am making a cameo for Chary. Before this I had been working on a keychain with the peace dove carved over a relief for Inés, and one with a cross for Alberto that turned out really nice. We also weave with the colorful thread from the towels. Last week, Nelly, who had been already released, approached my sister while she was waiting in line to bring us food and gave her a bag that turned out to be four burlap knitted together with a basting thread in which she had passed threads of many colors for our crafts. Sometimes, if the guard on duty is a little friendlier, we are able to send with her some of the pieces to our families.

Our artistic and intellectual activities sustain us and help us get through this imprisonment. Even so, we are often overcome by sadness and desperation. From our "subterranean isolation" that is this basement, we are visual and auditory witnesses to the manhunts these people engage in. We fall silent each time we hear them running to their cars, certain that they have obtained new information, or when we hear the sirens as they return, signaling that they have caught their prey, just as when they brought Alberto and I here. A few days ago we were sure that someone had escaped because they were chasing shadows all around with their guns drawn. Sometimes we listen to the radio if an inmate—while washing the chief's car, places it near the window so that we can listen to music.[19] For some reason the guard turns a blind eye and allows us to listen. That is also how we learned about the death of several *compañeros,* which is why we think that the radio also serves the double function of demoralizing us.

August 28

We were told a while back that after the last birth, which would be Gabriel's, we would be transferred to the prison in Villa Devoto, Buenos Aires. Two months ago three *compañeras* were brought here from Devoto to be tried by a military tribunal: Azucena, Patricia and Ana María. They are from Rosario and are very young, 16, 17 and 18 respectively. They are our window into the life that awaits us in Devoto. For the time being, Patricia loves the dubiously-colored broth with pieces of bone or the cornmeal with sausage that we can't even stand to look at anymore. She insists: "just wait until you get there and you will know what true hunger is." So we are mentally preparing ourselves and trying to appreciate the best of what we have here in light of our future hunger. Since the transfer order will arrive unannounced, we have already told our families. That is why Chary keeps pushing to get a marriage license for Alberto and me, because she is sure that once we are in the hands of the military in Buenos Aires, we will never get it and my family will not be able to take Gabriel to see his father regularly. She is coming to see me this afternoon and will give me the latest news on that.

August 29

Yes, they have issued the license. Which means...I am getting married! The wing is filled with laughter, jokes

[19] The Police Headquarters was also a temporary place of confinement for those non-political inmates involved in criminal activities.

and a bit of nervousness. Everything is so unbelievable that it feels like a scene from a surrealist movie. It makes me profoundly happy to have the papers, mostly for Gabriel. Who knows how long our separation will be and how long he will only get to know us and accept us as his parents through these periodic visits. I would have liked to have been allowed to have had a whole ceremony, either with Alberto being brought here or me being sent to Coronda for a day. But things are what they are and even though it is a marriage by proxy, we celebrate it.

September 5

Had these been better times, I would have been like any other bride, wearing a pretty dress and perhaps even a flower tiara. My current circumstances allow for much less than that, but who cares? I nevertheless am sporting a wide smile, my hair recently washed, wearing the best jeans that I have been able to acquire and the most showy sweater in the wing. I take Gabriel in my arms, who I have also dressed in his Sunday best. The *compañeras* bid us farewell amidst shouts of joy and I head out, proud of going to give this delayed "yes" that will join these two lives, suspended before an uncertain and threatening future.

September 15

The order has finally arrived: "Get your personal effects ready, tomorrow you will be transferred to Devoto." Did it really have to be on September 16th? We are kind of lost, scared and confused. Tomorrow will be the anniversary of the Liberating Revolution, or rather the military *coup d'etá* that overthrew Perón in 1955. It is not a good day for a transfer, especially if you take into account that most of the prisoners are peronists.

We try to suppress the paranoia but are still filled with suspicion and doubt. I hope they are unfounded.

Today is one of the saddest days of Tere's life. She has just given Eduardito to her mother and is now circling the wing trying to burn the spaces that she shared with her son into her mind. Juan Marcelo and Gabriel are coming to stay with us in Devoto until they are six months old, but Eduardo turns six months in eight days and it's not certain that Doña Ramona, his grandmother, will be able to make the trip to Buenos Aires to pick him up. Cristina is the oldest, but the military has allowed her to be transferred to Buenos Aires with her mother.

There is a lot of tension in the air. Not everyone will be transferred, only the ones who are on the list and a few who will be coming directly from the Intelligence Center. Of the *compañeras* I met when I arrived at the Alcaidía a good number are still here, but some have been freed and others have arrived over the last few months. My friends Tomasa, Norma and Stellita are no longer here. Mercedes, Marisa, Marta and Mirta arrived at the jail later, and I have become good friends with them.

We are scared because the unknown always frightens us. Perhaps this feeling will stay with us forever.

September 16, 6 a.m.

The wing's doors open and an undetermined number of women in blue uniforms (which is different from the brown color ones that the guards here wear) appear in front of us. Their faces and stares emit hate and their body language tells us that they are ready to attack. Then they start shouting and hurrying us along—get into lines of two, walk quickly to the bus, head down, hands behind your back. There is so much violence in each order, in their shoves and manhandling, and in their contorted faces that we are careful not to accidentally look at any of them in the eyes. Once we are on the bus, they force us to put our heads between our legs. Nené, Gladys and I lay our heads over our children's bodies as best we can. We take off to what we believe is the airport. An old military plane awaits us there and we board as we are once again shoved and yelled at and told to put our heads between our legs. And when the second act of this circus is about to start, one of the guards goes over to Nené and asks her to hand Cristina over. The guard is taken aback by Nené's violent reaction, which was completely in line with our situation. Nené stands suddenly, holding Christina tightly to her chest and yells: "¡Nooo! ¡No one is going to take my daughter from me! ¡Call the Commander, they told me I would not be separated from my daughter, go ahead, call them!" It is evident that the guard didn't expect such a strong reaction and she leaves to seek advice. Time has stopped at this moment and we await the outcome of the incident with our hearts in our throats, forgetting for a moment our current predicament. After a few minutes that felt like hours, one of the police officers in charge of the Alcaidía comes and makes Nené get off the plane with Cristina, saying that it is the order of the Commander. Soon after, the plane takes off. One of the uniformed women approaches me. She is about fifty years old, her curved nose makes her look like a hawk. She puts her mouth to my ear and says: "Son of a bitch, to come to have a child being a subversive." I only have eyes and ears for my son, what happens around me doesn't affect me. Gabriel has his eyes open and we spend the whole trip looking at each other.

September 16, 10 a.m.
We have arrived in Buenos Aires. Again we are rushed, shoved, and yelled at. In place of buses there

are several police vans. They take Gabriel from me and make me get in first. Then they return him with such an abrupt movement that I almost drop him. I am breathless, my heart beats vigorously. We are dispersed in the many vans, each one inside a tiny cell, and the trip starts again. I would like to look at the city through the window that is over my head but I have Gabriel in my arms and I would rather stay still since I have not gotten over the shock. He has been so well behaved and has not complained about anything. He is quite the little companion.

September 16, 2 p.m.
When they opened the doors of the van we were already in the heart of the prison. They made us get off and get into lines of two and then we were taken inside one of the wings. A photographer was waiting to take our admission pictures with identification numbers and fingerprints (I was lucky not to have lost them when I burned myself that day at the Alcaidía, otherwise I would have been in trouble!). Then we were examined by a doctor, for which we had to fully undress. This was the first humiliating experience, at least they never strip searched us at the Alcaidía.

Time passes slowly. Gabriel and Juan Marcelo whine; they are hungry and tired. We are speechless, there is still so much to learn since we are under a new regime and do not yet know its rules. But we have learned that these uniformed women are part of a shock troop that was trained for these types of situations: yes, they are called "requisition wardens" and we are going to have to deal with them from now on.

September 16, 5 p.m.
The bureaucratic part of our admission has ended. Gladys and I are set aside with our children and the rest

of the *compañeras* are dispersing. They lift their eyes to bid us farewell but they are not allowed to even grin. We watch them disappear with sadness. They are our family, our strength. The four of us are finally escorted by two uniformed guards. It is a long walk through terrifying hallways with gates that open and close as we pass. They stop us in front of a gate that leads to a rather spacious room. We now see that there are several people moving inside and we hear a baby cry. We have arrived at Hall 49, the prison nursery! As soon as we cross the threshold, two of them approach and hug us, sheltering us. Have we found a new family? Each of them is carrying a baby; both boys too. A third person waits farther away, there are three of them here. She is older and doesn't quite fit in this space for brand new mothers. We start exchanging names and making introductions. It has been an endless day and our exhaustion contrasts with the enthusiasm of the other *compañeras* who anxiously await news after months of incarceration. The problem is that Gladys and I can't give them any news because we too have been incarcerated for months. We talk a bit about our experience at the Alcaidía in Rosario anyway, and about the transfer and the others who came with us. Lidia has come closer too, and after greeting us has gone to make some food.

September 20

Hall 49 is huge and there are only five adults and four children (all of them boys). What a difference from the small room at the Alcaidía with 23 or more of us at a time! There, they had to put the bunk beds together so that we could all fit. Here there is a big pile of beds in the corner, only five of which are assembled along with the cribs. The wing is 50 meters in length and 20 in width. The beds are close to the bars—"so they can keep an eye on us during the night," the *compañeras* tell us—and the kitchen, bathrooms and the sink are at the other end. There are lots of windows with bars and lots of light shining through. The most important thing, however, is that the guards (who are not the same ones that perform the searches) do not harass us. After so many months of tension, this seems like an island, a vacation if you will.

September 21, 7:30 p.m.
There is a commotion and the door opens. A new woman appears in front of us; she is small with a big smile and a precious beauty in her arms—it's a girl! Yes, the family has grown and now we have Virginia and Evita. This time Gladys and I join the welcome circle, anxious for some news just like when we arrived a few days earlier.

September 29
I am slowly getting used to the changes, the new faces and this way of relating to each other and sharing parenting experiences. Things are calmer here. A guard we call Mongui has a son the same age as Gabriel and stops to see him every time she is on duty to compare their growth and tell or ask me about their differences and similarities. She is completely taken with my son's cuteness. While he is still less than three months old, if I say "one, two, three" and hold his hands, he stretches his legs and stands up. Even though he is so thin that it seems like his legs would not be able to hold him. There is also a German guard ("The Nazi," we call her), who is big—about 6 feet tall with a thick, detestable laugh and voice. She is young, single, and doesn't have children. Gabriel is her weakness, she stops by to see him every time she is on duty. She lifts him and plays with him. It makes me angry and jealous, and I wish Gabriel would stop smiling at the faces she makes. However, I

also know that it is better this way, that it helps our stay here for the next three months—to be a bit more normal.

October 5

There is a feeling of uncertainty in the air. This is the second anniversary of the assault on the Formosa military base by a Motonero command. We move about slowly and without making noise so as not to call attention to ourselves. One never knows with these people. Their revanchist attitude leads them to do the most absurd things. Even though we are somewhat protected due to being mothers, we will never be safe while in their captivity.

October 8

Susana has left with her baby...to freedom! The rest of us stay behind bars, with our hands raised in farewell, crying tears of joy and hoping deep down that this event will repeat itself for each one of us. The illusion also helps, though it is in constant tension with reality, it gives hope. We know that being separated from our children will be difficult: Gladys and I have been witnesses to Tere's intense pain. Who could remove this piece of themselves without bleeding endlessly?

Evita turns six months in two days but they are yet to grant her mother freedom. We must be prepared to accompany her in that moment of grief. Virginia tries to take things in stride, but we know what she is going through. Her anguish shines through her bright eyes.

October 10

Evita's grandmother is waiting in the guards' station. Virginia will be transferred today to another cell block for political prisoners. This moment is so different from the one a few days ago! We can't contain our sadness and, even though we try, we can't keep from crying as we walk them to the gate. Bye Evita, bye beautiful. The princess is leaving us, smiling like always, completely unaware of the separation and pain that awaits her over the next few days without her mom.

October 23

Now that Lidia has been freed, only Gladys, Juan Marcelo, Patricia, Martincito, Gabriel and I remain. The nursery seems cavernous but we feel at ease. The weather has gotten warmer and we sometimes fill the sink with water so the children can play. The food is good, for two reasons in particular: one of the prison's cooks strives to send us fresh food "for the babies" (though he knows that the mothers were the ones receiving the benefits of that food). Our families are also allowed to bring us some groceries like milk and eggs so that we can prepare healthy meals. Yesterday, for the first time, I had Gabriel suck on a piece of chicken bone and he seemed happy, though I doubt it was because it tasted good since he eats next to nothing. This worries me since he has only gained about five pounds in three months. The pediatrician who came to see him put me at ease by explaining that he is eating as much as he needs to sustain himself. Well, he apparently needs very little!

Juan Marcelo and Martincito have grown quite a bit and are beautiful. They are all well behaved but if we place them together, Gabriel always tries to take their toys. He is quite bold, especially since his adversaries are almost twice his size. I have placed a towel decorated with a colorful chicken at the head of his crib and, when he wakes up, he lifts his head and stares at the chicken for a while. It's fun to watch him observing the details so seriously. It only lasts a few minutes but I try to make his awakening pleasant, especially when I am not near him. He usually wakes up very early, around six, and stretches his arms to wake me. Then, I move him to my bed and my peace ends: he sticks his finger in my nose, eyes, and mouth while staring at me, as if telling me that I should be getting up. He doesn't know that we are only allowed to wake up at the sound of the whistle… perhaps he does know and he is taking advantage of the fact that he has me to himself for an hour.

October 27

The prison nursery is very harmonious. Gladys, Patricia and I are constantly chatting. We also take turns cooking and taking care of the children if one of us needs to rest. If someone feels down, the others give her a shoulder to cry on.

We are very busy and we wonder how much we would have been able to keep up the routine of a normal life along with motherhood. Patricia is the only one with that experience. At only 20 years old, she is the youngest of us and has a two year old daughter who lives with the paternal grandparents. We are amazed by her maturity. Her partner, who was 21 years old, was killed when they tried to escape their captors by jumping over to a neighbor's backyard. She remained kidnapped at a police station in the city of Buenos Aires for three months, while her pregnancy progressed in the confines of a humid and dark cell. She was subjected to mock executions by firing squad and had to survive endless humiliation from her captors. However, she lives every day with such intensity and joy that we are made to remember the importance of living in the here and now.

Gladys is also a strong woman, despite having a smaller, more delicate physique and dealing with a stomach problem that has plagued her for several years now. She, like her sisters, worked at the meatpacking company Swift when the military came to wipe out any suspected labor union organizing or talking of strikes.

In another month and a half Juan Marcelo will be taken from her, so she is now like Virginia, walking around the nursery trying to imprint these last moments with her son into her memory.

October 30

The *compañeras* from other cell blocks are brought out for recess regularly. As soon as we see them walk by the gate, we run to the laundry room and use a bench to reach the window. We start communicating with them very carefully. When Lidia was here we had access to newspapers and were able to keep up with current events. While we lack that now, the communication is ongoing. Some stand just under the window and pretend to have a conversation with each other, but they are really talking to us. We use this as an excuse to show them the children and they seem very happy about that. We don't know if the guard is aware of these maneuvers, but she usually doesn't bother us. And for us, who are pretty much isolated from the rest, this brief but periodic contact makes us feel like we are part of their lives.

November 2

Alberto has been punished without visitors in Coronda for almost two months. In order to get visitors there, family members of political prisoners must request a special permit. The jail is controlled by the gendarmerie, and the authorities there are absolutely arbitrary. They can delay that permit for as long as they want. After Alberto and I got married, my family submitted all the necessary papers to be allowed to visit Alberto. Finally the permit arrived and my mother will visit Alberto on November 5. Inés visited me today and has asked to take Gabriel to Rosario for a few days so he can see his father. It has been more difficult for me to agree this time because he is bigger now and I want to spare him the pain of a separation, even if it is a temporary one. On the other hand, as the days go by, I know that a permanent separation is approaching and I want to have every minute of the last two months with him. My sister's powers of persuasion win out again and I agree. She will be back for him tomorrow. I hurry to finish making a big bag that I have been embroidering a picture on and that says "my clothes." Gabriel is already sleeping, maybe he senses that a long trip awaits him.

November 3
Gabriel already knows his Aunt Inés. She has been here before with Aunt Beatriz to take him and Juan Marcelo to the hospital to get vaccinated. Though that trip was not enjoyable, there is something he likes about his aunt since he doesn't complain about leaving with her. Inés is so happy to have him in her arms that I join in that happiness and the separation is a bit less painful. I see them take off, Inés with the big bag that says "my clothes" over her shoulder and Gabriel smacking her face with his hands while laughing at his own mischief.

November 5
I wake up startled and remember: Gabriel must already be en route to Coronda with his grandmother. I miss him but I am thrilled to know that Alberto will get to enjoy having him there, at least for as long as the visit lasts. I have been told about the terrible conditions of the prisoners there. My experience right now in Devoto, which I know will end soon, seems like a luxury hotel compared to the terrible conditions that the *compañeros* in Coronda have. That makes me feel more at ease with having agreed to let Gabriel go on this trip.

Roll call has already happened and everyone is awake, including the babies. The guard has stopped in to tell us that something unusual has happened today.

Today of all days, the day of Alberto's visit! But it seems like the occurrence won't affect the visit. There was an earthquake at 5 in the morning that shook the entire jail. We can't believe it, we didn't even feel it. It is true, though. There was a considerable earthquake in Mendoza that was felt throughout this area of the country, including the provinces of Buenos Aires and Santa Fe.

When the guard leaves, I say: "It seems like the permit for Alberto's visit must have been miraculous, they had to move heaven and earth to get it!" and we all laughed.

November 7 at 6 p.m.

I approach the gate and I think I hear the German guard play with a baby. I look around the room and see Juan Marcelo and Martín. Does that mean Gabriel is back?

I get impatient because the guard still has him and I don't know how long it has been since he arrived. They finally bring him to me, looking very happy like someone who has returned from a long leisure trip. He recognizes me immediately and falls into my arms, which fills me with motherly joy.

November 18

The children are growing well. Our love, along with the relaxed atmosphere in the nursery provides them a certain comfort and stability. All three are adorable and we watch them with great amusement as they take turns stealing each others' toys in the playpen. They seem to get along and are kept busy. Gabriel likes paper. He enjoys the sound that the paper makes in his hands as he crumples it into a ball. Then he takes it to his mouth, which is when Mom appears to take it from him. He seems surprised and looks up at me because he doesn't understand why I would stop him just when he's getting to the best part of the game. Juan Marcelo is the oldest and commands respect. Martincito, on the other hand, is happy to just watch his friends.

I find myself getting jealous at mealtimes when Juan Marcelo eats all of his porridge and Martincito drinks all his milk. Gabriel, on the other hand, pushes his food around on the plate and blows on anything that comes near his mouth. There is no flying plane trick that helps—everything ends up either on the high chair or on the floor. Despite being so thin and small, he blows and shuts his mouth with surprising strength every time I try to feed him. I tried many recipes but he doesn't seem to care for his mother's culinary talents. Lunch and dinner always end the same way: a quick bath to clean the food off his body and then time to clean up the trail of food he left behind.

November 20

I have a visitor. Since we were transferred to Devoto, my aunt Josefa and my cousin Beatriz have taken turns visiting us once a week. I am lucky to have family in these parts, and they have not missed one visit since I got here. I must admit that I had not had a great relationship with my aunt and cousins in Buenos Aires due to the great distances that separated the two sides of my family since before I was born. However, it's been easy to establish a good relationship with them. Their periodic visits have been a small door to the outside through which I escape each week. They chat about a bit of everything. They tell me about the families, daily routines, plans for the weekend, and those farther into the future. My mother and sisters stay at their house whenever they come from Rosario and my aunt showers them with affection so as to help them through all the obstacles they might encounter when they visit me. Both mother and daughter are so sweet and adorable, and are great company during their weekly visits. They give me confidence, they give me faith.

December 3

The month of great expectations has started: Is the military going to publish a list of prisoners to be freed? Who will appear in that supposed list? Will I see my name on it? I am not the only one thinking this—almost everyone here and in other detention centers are probably thinking the exact same thing—because it is a legitimate expectation. We all know that we are at the whims of those in power and that they will also let us go according to their own whims. It is clear that in the face of this "great law" no other law matters.

Mom came to see me this afternoon with a big smile: this morning she went to the Italian embassy and her compatriots treated her very well there. Of course, they say, they would not allow the daughter of an Italian to be detained at the PEN without just cause.[20] This is why they have reassured my mother with the promise that they will intervene in favor of my freedom.

I have tried to convince my mother that the military does not give in easily—or ever—to external pressures, and not to not hold her breath. Though deep inside I hold a little bit of hope for this, too.

December 16

This nursery feels cavernous now, and our hearts bleed with every goodbye. Gladys and Juan Marcelo left today. Juan Marcelo was picked up by his father and grandmother and Gladys was transferred, like Virginia earlier, to another cell block. Their presence has remained, floating in the air. I have been with Gladys for almost ten months; through our pregnancies, the births of our children, and the transfers. She has always been very hard on herself, never allowing for weaknesses. She has an iron exterior that hides a gentle and generous heart. I wonder if she was aware of the great affection I have for her. I wonder what her nights without her son will be like and if she will be able to finally let go and cry.

December 20

We like that they let us out to the yard early in the day to avoid the heat later in the day. The backyard is right next to the nursery. But thanks to the absence of a roof and the possibility of seeing the blue or gray sky, as long as we get to see it, gives us a sense of freedom. We prepared a whole picnic! We take the strollers, a blanket to sit on and some sweets for the children. We miss Gladys and Juan Marcelo. They were an essential part of our group. The yard seems bigger and emptier.

I like to carry Gabriel on my back and run around singing "with my hobby-horse in hand, if he could trot that would be grand, and then trotting he could take me, to explore all of the land." Gabriel loves his horse rides and I have taught him to play patty-cake, so he happily slaps his open hands together. We only get one hour of recreational time each day, without exception. We would like for them to leave our gate open and to be able to go out as much as we want. But our status as political prisoners, or "terrorist detainees," the brilliant titles we have been given recently, has not been forgotten and we are not to be trusted. If they left the gate open, they would have had to leave a guard on lookout, so we are stuck with our daily hour. If it rains, we stay inside.

December 25

The expectations of many people, or at least of those who still had some, have evaporated today. We know from one of the guards that the list of prisoners to be freed has not been published. The military are probably happy to keep us here in their grasp. They doubtlessly think that we have not learned anything yet, and that despite the punishments we still pose a danger.

Today is a day of mourning in my country. Many Christmas tables will have one or more empty chairs. Some will be occupied again one day if we survive this test. But many will forever remain empty. That which we were years ago, the country I remember from my childhood, has changed greatly; so many wounds have been opened along with so much pain. It will take time, probably a few generations, until we can be confident again and until, perhaps, history can judge and punish so many abuses of power. How dearly we are paying for daring to defy an unjust social order, for challenging an economic order that brings so much exploitation and misery to our country, widening the gap between the rich and poor. I firmly believed, and still do, that it is possible to fight for a better world, for a more just and equitable society. I believed in my ideals and I joined my dreams to those of others, convinced as we all were that it was possible to build on the foundation of new values, values that centered human dignity, the right to work, and a full life without the pains of marginalization and social inequality. Since I was in high school I had worked in the more impoverished areas of my city. I have known the feeling of cold winters, in houses with dirt floors, where the dampness slowly penetrates through your feet. I have also known the heat of summer, when the shingles lining the roof are too thin to hold back the sun. I have seen families eat frybread as their main meal and hungry children without access to a school. And I have known mothers with tuberculosis who transmitted the illness to their newborns. But I have never seen any government officials visit those neighborhoods to learn about their needs and sadness.

Only a group of dreamers did it, I was among them, first out of charity, then believing in a political project. And they want me to regret what I did? What am I supposed to regret? I don't regret my dreams and ideals. This is why I sense that I still have days, months, even years ahead of me of silence behind walls, small cells, barred windows, and visits behind glass. Above all else, the time far away from my son, not seeing him grow, missing his first words and first steps. I know it will be hard, but I am confident and know that I can fight against all adversities, I also know that I will try to keep my integrity, and that I am not alone on this journey. Inside this prison and outside of these walls there are people that walk with me and support me, giving me strength and restoring my faith to me. I will be separated from Gabriel in a few days. I have no doubt that of all the pains I have lived, this one is going to be the worst, and I am afraid I might not be able to bear it. But Gabriel lights up everything with his presence and I am sure that his light and warmth will reach me regardless of where he is. Because there are no walls that can stop the dialogue of our hearts, nor silences that can prevent me from hearing the whispers of his voice in my ears. I will fall and get back up a hundred times, but I will never leave the road that will take me back to his light.

December 28

Elena, Chary and my two little dolls (Cecilia and Daniela) have come to visit. Their presence is so strong that I still hear their voices, laughter, and cries. Cecilia pays close attention to everything and she looks at her little cousin trying to guess the message in his body language, in his little agitated arms as he sees these two cute little figures in front of him. Daniela, who is only three months older than Gabriel, already wants to walk. She also responds to Gabriel's caresses by shaking her own legs and arms, and they both cry out in surprise and joy. My sisters tried to keep me up to date with the latest from the family, neighborhood, and country. They were trying to make me less isolated. Today, they told me that Nené, Juani, and Cristinita have been freed and my heart jumped with joy.

My *compañeras* of the prison nursery say that Gabriel and I are very lucky because in addition to the weekly visits from Aunt Josefa and Beatriz, every 15 days my mother or one of my sisters comes to visit. That family closeness makes this incarceration less painful.

January 1, 1978

It is the first day of an all-new 1978. Soon it will be the first anniversary of my kidnapping. I feel that I have lived so much, with such intensity in these past months. Some have been good experiences, like the times I've shared first with the *compañeras* at the Alcaidía then with those in the prison nursery at Devoto, and, more than anything else, Gabriel's birth. All the other experiences I would rather forget forever. On the whole, my experiences are still positive, because they have not been able to break my spirit or make me give up my ideals. I have learned that I know myself, my limitations—those things I can and cannot do, as well as those that I should and should not do. To be true to myself at all times, to follow my conscience, and to not accept any promise of help if it means giving up my beliefs. The new year starts its race today and I take off with it, hoping it means the start of the countdown for me.

January 6, Three Kings Day

Something extraordinary happened today and I refuse to believe that it was due to the intervention of the Three Kings. The story starts last night. Since it's summer, the sun doesn't set until late, at around

7 o'clock. During one of my wanderings around the nursery I hear chirping, like that of a sparrow chick, from behind the pile of beds. I get down on the ground and look from a distance while making chirping noises to see if it will come out of hiding. Silence, nothing moves. I chirp again but still nothing. I stop and move on.

This morning, Patricia and I got up and started making breakfast. After feeding our children, we placed them in the playpen so that we could eat. I sit on the left hand side of the bench and Patricia is almost next to me at the head of the table. We sit a while longer to chat since the heat is making every movement a bit slower. But life goes on beyond the heat and lockup, so we get up to clean. I start by sweeping around the table and I stretch a bit to sweep under exactly where I had been sitting only a few minutes before. Something heavy stops the broom. I think that it might be a toy and I drag it forward toward me and... it's a tarantula! I had to have been the one to find it, me, who suffers from arachnophobia! The spider's legs are curled up but its body is still about an inch wide. It is playing dead and I am paralyzed holding the broom and yelling for Patricia who is nowhere to be found. And before she appears, the huge spider stretches its eight legs and starts to run toward the playpen. I don't wait for Patricia; I hit it with the broom and in less than a minute it is truly dead.

One of the guards came by to tell us that the chirping was most probably the spider and finished her story by telling us that spiders scream when they sense a blow coming. This one in Hall 49, was very quiet, most likely because it didn't want to compete with my howls.

January 7

Beyond the scare that it caused us, the poor spider has turned into an emblem for us. We have asked to speak to one of the prison officials and argued that the presence of a tarantula in our vicinity is an even greater cause for concern due to the danger it poses to our children. For that reason, Patricia is having great difficulty staying alone with her son for two more months. I seize the moment to add that Gabriel has been having separation anxiety (which is true) and that taking him away from me in just four days could have negative consequences for his health. The deputy chief of security looks at us suspiciously but promises to look into whether they can delay the handing over of Gabriel to my family.

January 8

This small family is partying. We have gotten authorization for Gabriel to stay with us for fifteen more days; the spider must have interceded on our behalf. This means that my family will get him on January 26th and not the 11th.

January 18

The passing of time is something beyond our control. Despite that, the mind plays games and sometimes it seems like an hour has gone by when in reality it has only been a few minutes. Other times it goes by so fast that we are left halfway through a task because we don't have enough time to finish it. In my case, I am living in a great contradiction: I usually want time to fly by so that I can get out of these four walls as soon as possible, but today I want it to stop. The days, however, go by one after another with such speed that I can't believe that Gabriel and I only have eight more days together. I try to divert my attention from Gabriel and not to pick him up every time he asks because I think it will be better for both of us. That way we can both get used to not being there for each other. Is there any way to get used to that? We will undoubtedly overcome this test and survive the separation, but we will always have the bitter taste of this moment in our hearts.

January 25

I silently pack Gabriel's luggage: a red onesie, some socks, two jumpers—one made with nylon and the other wool—a pile of diapers, and two little shirts. I have added a checkered onesie that I made him and I put aside a blue jumpsuit for him to wear tomorrow during the trip. He looks at me from his chair. He has crumpled up a piece of paper I gave him and he throws it on the floor so that I pick it up and give it back to him—that is the whole game. But today Mom doesn't say anything, she indulges him and caresses his face every time she gets closer. Every now and again my eyes fill with tears. His eyes are locked on me and it's hard to believe that he senses something being only six months old. He must be caught off guard by my silence. So he stretches his arms and yells out so that I pick him up. I do it. I hold him against my chest and a great peacefulness floods over us. Then, he rests his head on my shoulder and I sing our favorite song: "Little brown eyes boy, if you ask for my life, my life I will give you. I will bring pieces of melon from the moon to sweeten your life." For a few minutes, as he falls asleep, we forget about the future and give ourselves over to this magical moment.

January 26

The guard approaches the bars and says: "Your family is here." Gabriel is in my arms, he has been in my arms all morning. I look for the bag with his luggage and walk very slowly toward the door. Patricia is next to me with Martincito and we both move as if a catalyst has befallen us. At the door, Patricia gives Gabriel a kiss and brings Martincito closer so they touch one more time. Then the guard opens the door and walks me to the end of the hallway where my mother is waiting with Ana. Aunt Josefa came with them but has stayed outside. We hug like that time in Rosario, only that at that time they were returning with Gabriel and this time they are taking him away. We can't find any words to speak. They know the pain this causes me and would like to be able to stop it. I look for comforting words, something like "don't worry, I will be fine," but I can't lie because I really don't know what my life without Gabriel will be like.

Gabriel cries, he just wants to be with me. He senses the tension even if he doesn't understand the outcome. I cradle him, I sing to him until he falls asleep.

It's a short visit since it's just for the retrieval of a child. The guard looks at me and says "it's time." Gabriel sleeps now, as if by dreaming he had decided to be my accomplice in order to make this moment less painful. I kiss him over and over. I kiss his eyes, hands, his small round head, all over his face and I hold him tightly against my heart. I fight back tears because I don't want to cause my mother and Ana more heartache. I kiss them both and hand Gabriel over to Ana, who takes him with infinite tenderness. I turn and walk away without looking back. I don't want to see them leave. I want to keep the last image of my son in my arms, I want to feel him next to me the whole time we are separated.

Part Three
My Diary[21]

> To my parents, for the time they are
> not with me.
> Gabriel

Thursday, January 26, 1978

I felt that something different was going to happen to me. I woke up and found that Mom's eyes didn't shine as before. Something gray dulled their usual green. She smiled at me but when I traced her hand over my mouth I noticed a crying tremor. She dressed me in the blue onesie with white footies. She lotioned and pampered me. She did everything slowly, as if her hands didn't want to move.

They called her. The sound of her steps was so weird! It was like millions of invisible, tiny strings were holding her back. Her arms held me tightly. Her body was tense. Only her heart, pressed next to mine, beat as if galloping with the wind to fly far away. There, at the end of the hallways, were my Lela and my aunt Ana. I didn't recognize them at first because lately I had only seen them from behind the glass. They hugged. My smiles were drowned in their many tears. I looked in silence, but later an intense pain, from deep inside, overtook me and I cried with the three of them. When we left Mom, I closed my eyes. I wasn't sleeping, no. I didn't want to see her. I know she didn't turn her head

---

[21] Fragments of "My Diary," written by my sister Chary Sillato, are interwoven here with the letters Alberto and I wrote to Gabriel. The letters are original, however, Alberto's were written after the diary was composed (between January and December of 1978) because he was only allowed to write to his son after May of 1979 when he was transferred from the jail in Coronda to a jail in La Plata and then to jails in Caseros and Rawson.

to say goodbye. All of a sudden I felt an infinite warmth, a caress that would never leave my skin, and I knew that we were not being separated, that would never be separated because we were made for each other.

When the last gate was closed and the last door locked me out, a bustle of people, air, birds, green, sun invaded every part of my body; it mixed with my blood and each one of them screamed that I was free!

Friday 27 at Aunt Josefa's house
I would have liked to have written last night, but I couldn't. As the sun set, slowly behind the houses and trees, when the birds flew back to their nests, I also felt nostalgic for my nest. All the anguish in the world became a lump in my throat. I started crying uncontrollably until I succumbed to sleep.

Saturday 28
If I had to describe everything, I would need a whole year to do so. It was the first time I traveled on a train. Yesterday the Retiro station was packed with people coming and going. Noise from the locomotives, so much noise. Noise everywhere. Noises that dazed me and drove me crazy. The train started to move, like an ugly giant with a belly filled with people that got smaller with distance. I knew that I was leaving my whole heart in Buenos Aires. The wheels kept repeating… you are leaving, you are leaving, in different voices but with the same tireless beat. My small soul filled with bitterness and sadness each time I heard it. Not even Lela's arms, nor those of my aunt, nor the sweet way in which they both talked to me, could turn off that unceasing sound that screamed of my time without Mom.

Rosario, 6 p.m.

Aunt Chary and Aunt Inés were waiting for us at the station. I was dazzled. I had never seen so many lights, so many cars. My mother was born in such a beautiful city! The city where she was happy, where on one random day she met my dad. The streets where Dad, with his big smile, kicked cans and told the stars that I was one of them, the most beautiful, inside of Mom. The streets where they strolled happily, hand in hand, while the breeze played with their voices and brought out the echo of my own voice from within Mom. I thought about so many things! How much of my parents' life has been embedded into my fantasy! How I would have liked to not be in this cab, looking out the window and to be a man, able to knock down prison bars, and with my fists break down those walls that I hate so much and give my parents back their freedom!

We get to the house. The house where I will live during the days that Mom and Dad are not with me. I am tired and before I feel the need to cry, I fall asleep.

Sunday 29.

It's raining. It's raining a lot. I had always heard the rain but never seen it before. Now I want to touch it and I press my fingers against the glass of the screen. The drops fall and fall. Transparent, beautiful. I know that they should be fresh and soft. The sky is gray, carrying heavy clouds.

I start to feel cold and scared. I hug Aunt Inés but it isn't the warmth that I know. At other times when I had been afraid, I sought out Mom and snuggled against her so that no one and nothing could hurt me. The rain and thunder don't hurt, I know that. Regardless, I want my mom. I look at Uncle Ernesto. He is a man! I tell him to give me courage to help me control this silly fear of mine. He understands my babbling and whistles a song.

My cousins do everything to distract me. María Cecilia asks me to play: "Gabel, Gabel," she calls me and brings her colored blocks, plastic wheels and a doll. Daniela watches me and smiles at me. She has almost the same color eyes as me. She seeks out my hand and squeezes it. My cousins are my friends. I love them. I am not as afraid anymore.

Monday 30

Last night Aunt Elena whispered to my ear that she prays to Jesus to return my parents to me so that Mom won't miss me so much. She is so nice! There is so much love in everyone! My Lela, my aunts and uncles, my cousins. The other day, while carrying me around Aunt Josefa's garden, Uncle Sebastián explained to me that my parents are wonderful and brave and that I should be proud of them. That, when I grow up, I have to write my story so that everyone can say "there goes Gabriel, who saw injustice first hand, who was breastfed between the walls of a prison, who gave his mother courage and strength and who alleviated his father's pain and suffering." Such wonderful words! My uncle is very wise and everything he says I hold near my heart so that this reality is less cruel and so that I feel less pain.

This afternoon, Aunt Charito was writing a letter to my grandparents in Corrientes. When she finished, she gave me the pen and I "added" a few kisses. I am so happy! Those were my first letters. If only Dad could have seen me writing! There are so many things my dad doesn't know about me. How painful it must be to know that he can't see me grow up. I heard that soon I will go visit him and I am saving up some antics for him.

We went to the post office to send the letter. I sat in the stroller. When we got to San Martín street, I was startled by the noise from the cars and the buses. I started to cry. I calmed down because Aunt Chary held me in her arms and whispered in my ear that she would not leave me in the middle of the hustle and bustle. Then, I decided to observe my surroundings: the very busy wide street, the old plane trees, the buildings, houses and businesses. This was the neighborhood where Mom grew up. The sidewalks that saw her play, ride her bike, the wicked curbs that dared her to "cross over to the sidewalk on the other side," the pizza shop where night after night, behind the counter, she asked for a slice of cheese in her softest voice. When we got back, we saw that Aunt Isabel and Aunt Sofía were there. They kissed me a lot and made me play and laugh for a while. I have written enough for today. Two or three yawns have drained my inspiration... See you tomorrow!

Tuesday 31

It is a beautiful evening. I can't describe with words my feelings of touching the depths of the sky with my eyes. To perceive the night reflected on my skin and to feel that one can be enveloped by the sweet, soft aroma of the fresh leaves and flowers without any prison bars in the way. It's wonderful to taste the silence, broken constantly by the song of a cricket, knowing that is not the same silence that I knew, imposed by the determination to punish. Rather, it is the silence of nature that is lulled to sleep as the shadows fall. I tremble. I don't know if it is the sudden cool air or just that I feel a nostalgic breeze run through my veins. What would Mom be doing now? I send her a kiss with each star and a hug in the doves' wings.

February. Wednesday 1

The days pass with lightning speed. Exactly six days ago at this exact hour I left Mom. I miss her, I miss her a lot. All the tenderness I have received does not replace the tenderness she had for me. I look around me. All the greenery that surrounds me seems colorless and dull compared to Mom's eyes. I stretch my arms trying to reach a pretty flower. I can't do it. I would have liked to have it in my hands to tell it of my sadness.

Hello Gabriel!

My dear boy: I am wondering what you are doing at this moment...looking at the sky, that sky the color of your eyes, or playing with your cousins, or listening attentively to what the canary is telling you from his cage with that beautiful look of distraction on your face. It was only six days ago that I held you in my arms, wanting to hold on to your smile, your hands in my face, your acute squealing and your tantrums. I miss you so, so, so much that sometimes at night, realizing that you are not by my side, I can't hold back my tears and I look for you in those moments of lonely silence. But then I smile again remembering your conspiratorial look when Mom would move you to her bed and you wouldn't let her sleep. Or watching you lying across your crib, trying to slip out through the railing. I try to get used to this new reality "without Gabriel" and think that all that love that I have for you will reach you through the wind, in the music, in my letters. And it will be Lela and your aunts who will hold and kiss you for me. Despite my sorrow I am not sad because I know that you are there, with your hands outstretched, waiting for Mom and Dad, who any day now will take yours in theirs. And they will start walking with you and sharing in your games. Because Mom has not yet explained to you that there is a brilliant sun waiting for us, that in spite of the walls and prison bars it shines through and illuminates us and warms us with hope and faith. Because your amazed eyes have yet to understand and your heart has already begun to suffer. But you will understand, I know you will. Though this letter now seems like a nice piece of paper filled with scrawls, good for crumpling and putting in your mouth, someday it will make you understand that Dad and Mom wish more than anything to be with you.

Don't be afraid, Gabrielín. I know that you miss me and that you too are looking for me and finding me a little in Lela's tenderness, in the walks that Aunt Chary takes with you for me, in that mother's heart that Aunt Ana hides deep within her, in the simple and generous way that Aunt Elena caresses you, in Aunt Inés' strong kisses, in Cecilia's sweetness and Danié's swagger. In the love that your uncles give you. This is not because Mom has all those qualities, of course not, but because in the long run nothing will remain of the times when Mom got upset because you didn't want to eat, or your moodiness. You little scoundrel, I wonder if you are behaving yourself!

Mom is well despite your absence. She is with other moms like your dear aunts Gladys, Tere and Lala, who can only think and talk about Juan Marcelo and Eduardito, and who remembers all your little tricks and charm fondly. They help me see that life is filled with joys and sadness, absence and separations, but that the beauty of life consists in finding the true sense of things and being able to see beyond the moment in which we live. And I see myself next to you and to all those I love. I see many other fathers and mothers hugging their children. I feel that there will be a blue sky of freedom for everyone.

My treasure, my little lion cub, you are with me and knowing that you are alive gives me strength and pushes me to move forward without hesitation or pessimism. I have wanted to write to you and tell you about so many things but my heart has gone on ahead and poured you all of this love.

I want you to tell Lela and your aunts that they don't have to worry about me, that you know Mom won't waiver, and the sadness won't overcome her. I want you to tell Dad that I love him very much, that I think about him all the time, and I know that we will be together very soon. I want you to ask Jesus, as Mom does every night, to be close to your heart and the hearts of all those little ones who are separated from their parents for a while or forever.

Gabrielito, I hope you never lose your smile or that naughty face or your curiosity to know everything. I hope you will grow up healthy and happy. Mom and Dad love you and need you.

Many kisses to Lela, your aunts, uncles, and cousins. And for you, all of my love and a kiss in your eyes. Mom.

P.S. Do you know? Martincito is leaving soon with his mom, isn't that wonderful?

Friday 3

Yesterday I couldn't write. I was sick and in a bad mood. What a shame that I couldn't enjoy María Cecilia's birthday party more! There were colorful balloons and a cake with candles. I liked the balloons. I liked to bite on them with my two teeth and feel their softness. I liked the sound they made when I squeezed them with my fingers. When the children started to play around me, I looked at them and was jealous of their happiness. Then I started crying inconsolably. Nothing made me feel better and nothing was enough. The balloons no longer mattered. The children ran around the backyard, the garden, among the trees and flowers. Their voices and laughter made me very sad. I would have liked to join the children and run around the places that knew of my mom's childhood. I so wanted to skate on the marble with them or let Greta, the dog, nip at my heels!

The party ended and my new friends left with their balloons, holding their mothers' hands. Then, just then, I realized the full extent of my loneliness. I started to cry again, so much so that the tears formed a river in my heart.

Sunday 5
Uncle Bachi, Ana, Elena, Inés, Chary, my cousins and I went to the park this afternoon. Such a beautiful place! We had lots of fun. We looked at the rides. Daniela and I wanted to touch everything while Cecilia was excited to get on the mechanical worm, the airplanes or the flying carpet. After that we went to the zoo. There were so many animals! Poor things, so big, so wild, begging from behind bars for a treat or some form of love. Humans are so selfish! We take away their freedom, take them away from their greenery, their skies, their suns, just so that we can gawk at them. Later on Cecilia and Daniela took a spin on the carousel. I fell asleep and woke up at home.

Tuesday 7
I went downtown with my aunts Inés and Ana and I am still exhausted. There were so many things to see! The window displays, the people, the toys! We got home around midday. Mom had told me about the soups Lela makes but I never imagined they would be this good. I ate an entire bowl despite being tired. For dessert I had a peach with dulce de leche. Then I took a good nap. It was already getting dark when I woke up. Why is it that one feels less protected at night? I was thinking about this when Aunt Charito's arms raised me up and held me tight, making me forget all of my "weird" thoughts.

Wednesday 8
Tomorrow I am going to visit Dad. I am in the playpen surrounded by toys. The poor things are on the

receiving end of all my anxiety. I throw them from one side to the other, I bite them, and every now and again they retaliate by hitting me in the head or face. I protest angrily and cry out. My aunts say that the sun is good for children and they leave me out half naked. It might be that the green from the plants and this feeling of being "sunbathed" are somewhat soothing my anxiety.

Coronda, Thursday 9

I am very angry and frustrated. I was absolutely convinced that I would be able to hug Dad when I saw him and give him my smile, my charm, and the ocean of kisses that Mom gave me for him. But none of this happened. As we waited to be let into the jail, people looked at me and fussed over me saying "such a beautiful boy," "so charming," "such a big boy."

Little was left of that charming boy as soon as we crossed the threshold. I don't know if this is all because of a girl who started crying (which led me to cry) or if I was already brimming with tears that suddenly spilled out of me. The fact is that no one and nothing could sooth me. Dad looked worried. He imagined thousands of things that could have caused me such anxiety. I tried to tell him, unsuccessfully through my tears, that I loved him as much as he loves me, but he didn't understand. He didn't get my desperate attempts at showing him the enormity of a son's love.

Dad! Young Dad, with his aged soul. My dad, who I have and at the same time don't have. One day, Dad, you will hold me and I will hold you under an infinite free blue sky and together we will begin a life of whistles, of soccer balls, of bicycle kicks in the little kids' soccer field, of watching cartoons. It will be filled with all these marvelously simple things that make one a man.

Monday 13

I just know that they said: "sanctioned." It was as if I had been punched in the gut. My aunts Josefa, Beatriz and Chary started to cry but I held back.

Dearest Mom. I want to see you so much! Mom, your little prince is strong and very brave. I am what you taught me to be: a brave boy! Mom, don't be discouraged and don't suffer. I am your ray of sunlight, who illuminates your cell from the outside. Don't cry Mom, because now I am crying for you.

Tuesday 14

I am very sad. As hard as I try, I can't find anything to distract me. I want Aunt Chary to hold me all the time. It's the only way to take the pain after yesterday's disillusioned news.

Wednesday 15

Uncle Sebastián is here for a visit. The truth is that I think he came to see me. Since he saw that I was so sad, he took me for a ride in the stroller around the neighborhood. He said that that would distract me. It was true! As we walked around he showed me this and that and made me laugh. He spoke lovingly and tried to cheer me up in the face of much anxiety. We get along really well and are good friends. We just love each other so much, and that's what matters.

Friday 17

I didn't realize how much I missed Lela until I saw her last night. I was so happy to be in her arms! Today she made me a tasty meal; I feel better when she feeds me. We sit on the porch or in the backyard and she shows me her plants and flowers and lets me play with them. She brings me closer to Gabrielito's cage (my canary). As I try to touch him from outside the cage, Lela laughs. Every now and again all the distractions, the baby food, and the desert make me think that I might just be as spoiled as they say I am. María Cecilia stopped by. I showed her my new skills and she celebrated each of them gracefully.

Monday 20

It is 2.30 on this radiant and warm sunny afternoon. I can't sleep. Lela and my aunts are trying in vain to get me to rest. I think I am going through an acute case of "being a mama's boy." Aunt Charito carries me in her arms around the backyard. I am getting to know every plant rather well. So many colors! There is a small tree with lots of small lilies. A beautiful butterfly flies in between them. I look excitedly and smile. It is the first time I have seen a butterfly. I follow its path with my eyes. It is so vain! It moves its little wings, poses every now and again and disappears between the leaves.

Friday 24

I went to Eduardito's and Juan Marcelo's house. It felt strange to share so many things with them: games, laughter, punches, babbling and a giant sky without barriers. Yesterday we were compañeros in a place where the sun was given to us in small daily rations. Now we are united by the great pain of absence. We know the same astonishment, the same fear, the same loneliness.

Sunday 26

I woke up very late. In the afternoon, Chary gave me a nice bath and we went with Inés to visit my aunts, Isabel and Sofía. I love to take strolls, to see all the cars, people, lights. I open my mouth, smile along with everyone and show off my two teeth. I look through the window and hop like a toad. I think I have gotten used to (or adapted, as the adults would say) my new lifestyle without great difficulty. My surroundings are new to me. I learn to tell things apart, to enjoy the colors, the air, and the thousands of different sounds, but more than anything I am learning about a world completely different from that which was my world for so many months. A world surrounded by cold and hostile walls, but nevertheless incredibly sweet because it was my world with Mom.

Tuesday 28
Mom! Your eyes filled with tears. You thought your little lion cub had forgotten your face, your voice. There is no pain that can stop your smile nor microphone that can change your songs. My dear mom, all mine, with a thousand larks in your fingers to caress mine. Mom, whom I recognize from other faces because I am your voice, your laughter, your joy, your gestures, your eyes, your sun, your day, I am your own image!

10 o'clock at night
I can't sleep. I close my eyes. Along with the night sounds are the songs that my mother sang to me this afternoon. I felt her caresses, even though her hands couldn't reach me, and her kisses were lost in the silence. They reach me now like a shaking rattle that grazes my forehead and leaves music and tenderness in my heart.

March. Wednesday 1
I was excited all morning. We left Ezeiza around noon. I ate very little. Lela bought me a flan at the Devoto bar. My first meal out! How yummy! Lela watched me, entranced. I, on the other hand, looked from the restaurant's window at the front of the jail. It gave me a terrifying feeling and made me anxious. I thought that if it was up to me, I wouldn't even try to cross the street to

go near it. I go, however, because Mom is there waiting for me. It's a heavenly hour…

Thursday 2
I cried a lot this afternoon. I couldn't stand one more moment seeing my mom in the visiting room. I so wanted to hug and kiss her. I started flailing and yelling. Nothing could soothe me. I was sure that I had grown up enough that I could destroy everything with my fists, but I was wrong. I am so angry that I don't recognize myself.

Saturday 4
I have little to tell. I am eating well and sleeping better. Though I completely distrust the nebulizer, I see that they are not all that bad. Mom was also feeling better. I left her feeling very bad on Thursday, but she went back to her usual energetic self. I am happy. I show it by jumping and squealing. It's not for nothing that Mom calls me "her little frog."

Sunday 5
Every day has been warm and sunny. It is about 10:45 PM and we are heading to Rosario. Lela, my aunt, and I sleep a lot. Aunt Ana and Aunt Inés were anxious to see us and hear news of my mother. I looked around at everything and laughed a lot. I am getting used to returning home.

Monday 6
I got a letter from Mom. It is the most beautiful letter in the world. It has thousands of suns, moons, stars, skies, birds, flowers… But more importantly it is filled with so much love that I wondered who of us was in the letter and then immediately understood that it was all

of Mom, and all of Dad, and all of me. The three of us together, very close together.

Hi Gabriel!

My son, is it true what they say? That you have not forgotten me, that even though this forced separation is trying to erase our ties, you have not forgotten that I am your mom? Today, when our eyes met, yours told me about your pain and impotence. There was awe in your eyes and in your half-open mouth. We've had moments of profound closeness: you drank your milk snuggling in my arms while I sang "Hush, little baby, don't say a word Mama's gonna buy you a mockingbird And if that mockingbird won't sing Mama's gonna buy you a diamond ring." Then we looked at each other and could see past our eyes, into our souls, where my love found yours. Today we overcame time and distance, and I know that nothing will be able to keep us apart. From your Aunt Chary's arms, you turned and looked deep inside me, almost without blinking, while you drank your milk, and I from this other shore sang our favorite song to you. My sweetheart, you are in me and I feel your strength rise from my heart, filling every inch of my soul. I love you, Mom.

Wednesday 8

"Happy birthday Aunt Ana!" I say with a bit of a cold. My eyes are shining and red and I have a slight fever. I think I am going to stay in bed today.

Monday 13

I went to Andresito's house. He is Marisol's son. We made a good mess. I liked playing with him. If our houses were closer we would be able to share toys. He is a tall baby, thin with big clear eyes filled with mischief. Deep down, we both know we need each other. I hope that as time goes by we become good friends... great friends ... true friends.

Thursday 16
When I am with Ceci and Danie I have no time to write. I drool as we play and play, and it makes me happy. My other teeth don't want to appear. My gums bother me a lot so I bite on anything I can find. I accidentally let out a cry and Ceci ran to the phone, dialed and "talked" to Mom: "Aunt Carmen, Gabelito is crying, come soon," she said. I looked at her while sucking on my thumb and a cookie. Danie, on the other hand, ran around the table. Everyone in the family is trying to teach her a different sound from the ooh, ooh, ooh that she says but it has been impossible. Since it is already late, we have been lined up to go to bed but we have not given up. We are something else!

Saturday 17
A letter from Mom. I want to kiss it but I bite on it instead. It says so many nice things! I am happy with my Lela, my uncles and my cousins but I wish I was with Mom.

Hi Gabriel!

Hello my darling! You know what? I think that you are going to come visit me soon. You will get on a train... chugga-chugga-chugga-choo... you are going to get here and we will see each other. Hello Gabriel! I am going to say and you will blow me kisses.

But, you know what? We won't be able to touch each other now because there is a glass partition, like the other window, that neither of us can break. But we will play just the same, hide and seek, and talk...Hello, hello, hello! we will say through the handset and sing "the wheels on the bus go round and round, round and round" and "hush little baby..." Daddy is also waiting for you to visit and play with him.

Gabriel, Daddy and I love you until the end of time and want to be with you. But we don't yet have the keys to get out of here. One day the doors will open and we will go with you to the merry-go-round in the park. Would you like that?

Gabriel, my love, I am sending you tickles on your feet and a kiss on your nose. I love you, Mom.

Sunday 19

It's 11:55 AM. The sun peeks out from behind the clouds like a shy little boy. It's cold but Chary wants me to take advantage of the fresh air so I am in the yard. I am now eating a piece of bread dipped in soup, something my Lela does. I love her so much! When she walks by I lift my arms and let out a cry. I love it when she carries me in her arms and sings me old songs, like the ones she used to sing to my mom.

Aunt Chary placed me in front of a mirror. She does it all the time because she knows that I like to laugh looking at myself. But today I saw myself a lot bigger. How I have grown! If Mom and Dad could see me now! When I think about the fact that they can't enjoy every one of my milestones, my pain is as vast as the sea.

Monday 20

At around 7 this morning I discovered the letter T and started making the sound of words I liked with it: TETE...TA TE... ETA. I crawled around the bed, banged on the headboard with my little hands and laughed at my own mischief. In the afternoon, my aunts Anita and María came to the house. They love me very much. They brought me two beautiful overalls that they made themselves, so Chary dressed me like a "big boy" and we went to wish Danié a happy birthday. We played endlessly with her and Ceci on the floor and on Aunt Elena's bed. Uncle Ernesto kept testing us and Elena said that my eyes shone brightly the whole time. I was very happy today, even though I received a rather sad letter from Mom! I am going to send her lots of hugs and my new sounds in every ray of sun so that every inch of her is filled with my love.

Hola Gabriel!

My darling: I just received your beautiful letter that came to fill this gray, rainy afternoon with light and joy. So many things to tell! You are growing so fast! I was reading and thinking about you in each of those situations: with your toys, with Lela, taking a walk with Aunt Chary. I miss you so much, my dear boy. Will I ever be able to get used to being without you? Every time I start a letter I think about how much you helped me write them and how easy it was for both of us to write them to Lela and to your aunts. Our letters were as long as the one I just received. Do you remember our glorious times at the nursery? The first time I went to the yard and had to pass by all the places where we used to walk together, the memory of us looking at the sky, the ducks, or picking flowers for Juan Marcelo and Martín brought tears to my eyes. It hurts, Gabriel, it hurts more than anything in this world to be separated from you. But don't worry, these moments come and go. When I get out of those trances, I find affection and understanding in so many other mothers who are far from their children, and I feel better and start making plans for when we are together again.

Right now I am hearing the cry of a baby that you and I know too well. I am not making this up, would you believe that MARTINCITO and his mother are on this same floor, just two wings away? I still can't believe it, it is as if a part of you is there too. They have been here since Thursday and I had the chance to see him that same afternoon when I was giving out the bread. The reunion was beautiful and I gave him a big kiss for you. When I first started hearing his cries so close by, I got really sad because it reminded me of you, but now I love hearing him laugh and cry. The presence of a baby can transform this place.

We were moved on Thursday morning. We were tidying up when the guard came in and told us to get our stuff ready. We were a bit sad because we didn't know where else they would take us, and because we had grown to like each other and were afraid to be separated. This morning we were taken to mass and I prayed for all of those who had died recently and those who are suffering right now.

I am now in another cell block with other compañeras *who are also nice, but I still miss the others.*

My baby, my cutie
I want to send you
A good angel
Like the one who takes care of children
When Mom is not with them.

I send you lots of kisses, caresses, smiles, and songs in each ray of sun and in each star. As many as you sent me in each drop of rain. Mom.

Tuesday 21

It's past 1:30 in the afternoon. I am on the kitchen floor playing with a bunny. I go back and forth with the poor thing, which is already missing an ear, part of his head and hardly has a tail left. I have discovered the kitchen cabinets and the stovetop. I hang from the knobs, bunny in hand, while opening and closing them to show off my skills and strength...

I stopped writing because something very interesting happened: Lela came with a vanilla pudding cup.

I love her so much! She knows what I like and spoils me rotten. She proudly takes me and walks me from the house to the street corner. I hug her and caress her and show all of my affection.

Wednesday 22

I took a very short, short nap. Chary almost lost her mind when she heard me talking because it had taken her over an hour to get me to sleep! I was chatting non stop with my dear blue bear. It isn't mine, Danié got it as a gift, but since it's on top of the table with the light, I've learned, first to know him and then to make him a great friend. I kiss him, bite him, pull his arms and legs, his nose, and throw him on the floor and talk with him. He answers with soft caresses.

My cousins are awake. Ceci runs towards me with her arms stretched and saying: "Gabel! Gabel" She has such a sweet voice! Daniela, on the other hand, walks forward slowly with her pacifier in one hand and her sandals in the other. She looks at me and smiles. She stops at the door of the bedroom and calls to me, "oooh... oooh." She is so pretty! I almost fall out of the bed in my attempt to get closer.

Friday 24

A letter from Mom! Lela shows it to me and says: "Who would have written to Gabriel?" I want to answer "Mom!", but I can only say "ba-ba-ta-ta." It's so frustrating! Lela smiles at me. She has read in my eyes that I understand. I am happy. She opens the letter and starts to read in that wonderful voice that brings me so much peace.

Hello Gabriel!

I am going to tell you something nice that happened today: we went to the yard and what a surprise! Patricia and Martincito went out with us. It was so wonderful to be able to hug each other, talk, and stroll together. Martín looks more like you every day: he is more restless, observes everything, and moves around more. Did you teach him that when you were together in the playpen, talking in that language of looks and cries? Such a little scoundrel! What I would give to see you again next to Martincito, giving him some of those loving slaps of yours.

I think of you all the time. I remember your last visit, looking at me with your big eyes behind the glass, waiting for me to lift you in my arms and, maybe, asking yourself why Mom didn't do so. My treasure, some day Mom will explain and you will understand and see that she suffered as much as you did.

I want to see you so much, but I also want you to go see Dad to bring him all the love you and I have for him, and give him joy and strength. Please don't cry because then he gets sad.

Gabriel, Mom loves you to the moon and back. Many kisses, Mom.

Wednesday 29

We left home early. It was still dark. Lela and my aunts told me that it would be a beautiful day. Coronda is already a familiar place to me. I even like it. Behind the big walls and that green gate is my dad. Before going in, Lela and Aunt Ana told me that I should behave like a little gentleman. They seem to forget that I have grown up. That is why, when I saw Dad through the glass, my heart started beating faster and my smile was wider than usual. Everything that I know, that I have learned lately, fought their way out of my hands and mouth. There was Dad, drowning my gestures with his eyes. He said such sweet things through the handset that I wanted to snuggle against him and never let go. When the visit ended, I didn't want to leave and started whining. Lela made me say goodbye with my hand. Dad got closer, put his hand on the glass and looked at me with sadness. I know what he said: "We are men!" And, like him, I pressed my lips together and swallowed my tears.

April. Sunday 2

I woke up ready to get into all sorts of trouble. I'm wearing a striped t-shirt, red pants, and sky blue shoes. I walk around the backyard holding onto the railing. Every now and again I lean over to pick up a fistful of dirt or tear up some leaf.

We went to the bus station with Aunt Chary to pick up Aunt Juani. I had lots of fun on the bus. I stood on the seat, jumping and crying a bit. I wanted to touch everything that I saw through the window. The ticket collector played along and said that I was very clever adding: "What beautiful eyes!", to which Chary answered: "they are his mother's," and he said: "She must be very pretty then." My clothing felt tight at that moment.

Wednesday 5
HAPPY BIRTHDAY MOM!

It's 5:25p.m. and I am just waking up from my nap. In a little bit we will go to Fernando's party. I know I will have a lot of fun but I would have liked to be celebrating another birthday...yours, Mom! Not with balloons but with a huge chocolate and dulce de leche cake, helping you blow out the candles or slapping at the frosting with my hands. But, as you know, I can't give you any of those things, so I send you with this fall wind that is blowing like crazy, this "ma...ma...ma" that I started saying today, just today, so that you feel like the happiest birthday girl in the world.

Daniela, just to make fun of me, has started saying m...m...ma today. She is so cute and funny, with the gap in her teeth and sweet smile. I am alone. The Fiorella girls went with their fathers. I was dressed in a white pajamas, took a bottle, and am now heading to bed; but before that I want to tell Mom that I miss her and I ask her to hum every night in her heart and in silence that song that she taught me when we were together. Her voice will reach me in the song of a cricket, or in the reflection of the moon, or in the mischievous eyes of the stars, or in the tenderness of those sparrows that take refuge in the molding of the columns on the front porch when the sun sets. It will reach me and I won't be alone.

Wednesday 12

I am dirty from head to toe. I have crawled all over the house. Cecilia and Daniela play with me.

Today is Dad's birthday! A kiss from me would make him so happy! Since I can't do that and he can't hold me in his arms, I send a kiss with this sparrow that is flying through the leaves of the orange tree. I am sure they will take it to him because sparrows, though mischievous and scoundrels, are also extraordinary.

Thursday 13

I have learned something: Zulema taught me to say "bye." I move my hand (well, the truth is, most of the time I move my entire arm).

Friday 14

I am very happy to be learning new things everyday. Since they taught me to play patty-cake and to say bye, I've been rehearsing all the time. I have also learned how to move my hand when they sing "what a cute hand" like my mom taught me. I am sitting in the playpen. Lela is talking to me and I answer with soft cries. I am a bit sleepy. I think Chary will sympathize and take me to bed.

Uncle Sebastián arrived this afternoon, always with his wisecracks: he pushes my walker and celebrates my tricks. I say things like "da...ta...pa...te" and he says that I am very smart. What an uncle!

Saturday 15
Lela went to visit Mom and I miss her. This morning we received a letter from my grandmother in Corrientes saying that Dad sends me a thousand kisses. Even though they are not with me, I am very happy to know and feel that my parents love me so much.

Tuesday 18
A letter from Mom! It came with a gift for me: a bunny that moves its arms and legs if I pull the string on its back. I am so happy when a new letter arrives! I was a bit sad because Lela is in Buenos Aires, so the letter and the bunny cheered me up. I play with Serafín while Aunt Chary reads me the letter for the second time.

> *Hello Gabriel!*
> *Hello my love! I am sending you my friend Mr. Bunny. Do you know his name? Serafín the Bunny...*
> *The bunny Serafín*
> *Jumps and runs in the garden*
> *Greets Mrs. Parrot*
> *While he eats a carrot*
> *Hello, what are you up Gabriel!*
> *Do you want to eat, too?*
> *I will give you a little piece*
> *And you will play with me a little bit*
> *Gabriel, I give you Serafín so that you can play with Cecilia and Daniela. I love you very much, Mom.*

Wednesday 19

It's 3 in the afternoon. Chary was set to nap for a while but I interrupted her. I started playing in the bed and then asked, by shouting, for the bottle. She drank some mate but, since I was crying in the stroller, she had to stop. She looked at me earnestly and said: "this is the second interruption! I'll show you!" But I knew she was kidding so I laughed. I am now sitting on her lap and rehearsing what I've learned:

ah..ba...ta...te..me..ma..pa.. Every now and again I would cough to appear important. I have a pen in one hand and I write on the table. I bite the block that my aunt is writing on, I hit it, I throw it on the floor, and my aunt gives me kisses. I sneezed a few times and - since Chary kept saying "epa, epa!" —I started to clap my hands.

Today I got my first letter from Dad. I am a very happy baby!

Dear son:

How are you? I am well, better when I can write to you. How is grandma? Give her a kiss for me, and to your aunts too. I am also going to ask you about someone you love very much. Well, someone we both love very much: Mom! Yes, I was asking about her. Give her lots of kisses from you and me.

Tell me, is it true that you have a small radio and listen to it all day; that you sing and dance when they play music? I can picture how you look: messy long blonde hair, a round face, mischievous eyes, dirty hands and face from playing in the yard, a shirt that is a bit too big, and pants that are falling off your big, round, uncovered tummy... tough break for your grandma, having to pick you up constantly. You take advantage of the fact that grandma is busy in the kitchen and carry the radio under your arms while you run around that small world of rooms; opening drawers, dropping things everywhere, while she asks: "Gabriel, where are you? What are you doing? Don't break anything!" Tell me the truth, you like breaking things, right? Tell me if you have broken anything important and if your grandmother and aunts were upset. Try to be less destructive. When you are nervous, don't throw everything within reach. I remember one visit when you were in a bad mood and you wanted to go home so you started hitting your aunt. Do you remember? I think that you are very nervous. I want to be your friend and play with you, if you want. How does that sound to you?

One day, when we are together again, we will go on walks like friends. Mom will be there too and the three of us will have lots of fun and have ice cream. Do you like ice cream? I like it too. Which flavor?... Ah! Chocolate and cream, just like your mom. I prefer strawberries... Yes, I will give you some... We will also go to the park... and we will buy candy and sweets... And, no cigarettes for you Gabriel, cigarettes are for adults, like me...

Anyway, if you want you can invite your cousins but not to fight, ok?

Any day now, soon, I will be with you. I love you very much, Dad.

Thursday 20

I realize that each day I am growing, and growing a lot. I am wearing overalls with chickens on it (Aunt María, who lives in the countryside, embroidered it), a jacket and white shoes. It looks like I am going to daycare. I learned something today. Chary took me to the backyard and taught me to "touch" the sky. It's wonderful to feel that my fingers can be filled with blue and with the sun. But it's amazing to know that I can caress a passing cloud and that, since it can go anywhere, it will carry my caresses in its body of rain and cotton, and will drop them softly on my mom's face or my dad's hair.

Sunday 23
Chary was showing me the moon last night. It was so round and pretty that I wanted to touch it, take it, and keep it for myself. I wanted to fill the pockets of my overalls or my jacket with its smile. We went to Elena's house and Cecilia ran to meet me but Daniela threw herself on the floor and cried (uncontrollably jealous). I have concluded that we love each other "to death": she steps on me, then hugs me until I choke, then throws toys at my head, if I am sitting on the floor she sits on top of me… and after all of that comes the fits of jealousy. She finds a favorable place, very close to Elena or Ernesto, throws herself facedown on the floor and lets out a heart wrenching cry (though my heart doesn't feel a thing!). I fight back: kicking, pulling her hair, pushing; but that's not enough. When I see her approach again I move away without a second thought or I start to cry.

Cecilita, on the other hand, is all sweetness. She doesn't know what to give me or how to pamper me, though last night she made a mistake that left my lower lip completely swollen, poor thing. She wanted to pick me up and… boom! I fell on my mouth. I bled a little, enough for my aunts to rush to my side, followed by my cousins. When I stopped crying, I realized what had happened and was very happy: this was my first time getting hurt! I am becoming a man!

It's a bit cold. Ana is sweeping the porch and I follow her hurriedly with my walker. I secretly pulled a fern leaf and tried to eat it but Chary saw me and said: "Chanchón, give me that!" I spit it out and laugh.

May. Wednesday 3

It's past 10:30 p.m. and Chary and I just got home from Aunt Elena's house. I was deeply asleep but Ana woke me up to tell me that the mailman had come this morning and brought this beautiful letter from Mom.

Hello Gabriel!

Hello my big boy! Have you been behaving? Tell me, Gabriel, did you show Renato the duck to Dad? And now, where did you put it? What did Dad say? Did he play with you?

When you come back to see me we won't be able to touch and hug each other because of the glass, but we will be able to play. Bring your handkerchief and we can do magic tricks!

Gabriel, I love so, so much. When they let me go free and I can be with you, we will go to the park to play and ride the merry-go-round.

Bye my love. Kisses and more kisses, Mom.

Thursday 4

Surprise, surprise... a new tooth! Lately I have been eating lots and taking peaceful naps. Aunt Anita came and brought me a beautiful shirt. It fits so well! Then, as we usually do, Chary changed me and we went downtown... I had lots of fun. I loved the lights, the noise and the window displays. I never know what to look at first! I slept a bit, but woke up when we were on the Córdoba pedestrian walkway. We stopped at the Plaza Sarmiento to look at the fountain. I heard the sound of the water flowing and clapped. We took a bus back to the house. I decided to sing as loud as I could. Every now and again, the driver looked at me through the rearview mirror and winked. I didn't notice at first but when I did. I sang him a "song." He waved when we got off. Aunt Anita was so proud that everyone looked at me that she told Lela and my aunts when we got home. I felt very "popular."

Friday 5

Aunt Chary has been calling me "Bichinuchi" from the moment she unlatched the front door. I don't know where she got the nickname. She picks me up and gives me tons of kisses. Then she plays the bad cop, like now and "dares" me because I don't want to sleep anymore.

We are sitting on the bench on the porch. We observe the plants. There are so many corals! The orange ones have started to tan due to the autumn sun. I also see the "birds of paradise." There are three of them and are an intense orange color with a purple center. They are so beautiful! I realize why Lela likes plants so much. They are so pretty and fill our hearts with this multi-color tenderness... Lela and I are in the back. I watch the parrots and "Gabrielito" while eating a piece of bread soaked in mate. I can't stand being away from Lela for too long. She can calm my anxiety and she fills me with hugs. She is mom when I want mom. Since it is time for my baby food, I sob a little... I had noodle soup. Now, Inés gets me ready for bed, dressing me in a onesie with little drawings. She washed my face, my hands, ears ... and my tail! My aunt, she makes me laugh so much! I am happy... happy...

Tuesday 9

My grandma Lorenza sent us a letter to let us know that Aunt Martha will go to see Dad this time. We were supposed to visit him but only one person is allowed per visit. I am disappointed. I really liked the thought of seeing Dad. It would be so nice to see him, smile at him, hit the microphone with my hand, play patty-cake!... It's almost 6 p.m. and Lela sits me on the countertop and gives me bread with butter soaked in mate. That I do like! I kick my feet happily and laugh, showing all my teeth. Chary ruffles my hair and combs it back and says "wire cape" because of my curls, like Greta. Ana gets angry because she says that that ruins my natural look. Inés hugs me tight. My grandma gets angry because my aunts' "affectionate gestures" are going to make me choke or drop the mate. Even Greta participates by jumping and making her vaccination tags jangle ... I am in Chary's arms looking through the glass door that leads to the porch. It was a pretty day and now a sort of blue shadow falls over the garden. It's serene; the warm humidity of this hot May night makes everything feel a bit dreary. The stars are beginning to make their marks on the night sky. It is said that the stars are small windows through which God watches us. I look for one and smile at it. God knows that my heart asks for Mom and Dad. Anita was talking about Inés' wedding yesterday and said: "Gabriel will represent Carmen and Alberto, as if all three were there." That is true, for everyone else I am a bit of both of them, but I still want them by my side, I need them.

Wednesday 10

I said "dad." I was so happy that I applauded myself. Later, my whole family congratulated me. It's wonderful to be able to name the man who is part of the sun and the wind to me.

Thursday 11

I got a letter from Mom. It has a green envelope and stamps. I try to reach for it while Aunt Inés reads it because I want to kiss it... well really I just want to bring it to my mouth and chew on it.

Hello Gabriel!

Let's play with the dry autumn leaves.. cric-crac... do you hear the sound that the leaves make when we step in them? And we jump... cric-crac, cric-crac, cric-crac... and we run... cric-crac, cric-crac,cric-crac ...

Shsss! Do you hear, Gabriel? Ushhh, ushhh! It's the wind coming to play with the leaves. It blows them off the ground and carries them higher and higher and then they fall back to the ground.

Look, Gabriel! How beautifully the dry leaves dance! Do you want to dance with me and the dry leaves? Let's go find Cecilia and Daniela to play with us.

Gabriel, my treasure, my life, I offer you all the autumn leaves to play with, and a bunch of hugs and kisses, Mom.

Friday 12

Today is Aunt Inés' civil ceremony. It's a hot and humid day. Cecilia, Daniela and I started our mischief early. At around 10 a.m., Bachi, Inés, Elena, and Bachi's parents went to the town's clerk and returned around 11. We were happily waiting for them and applauded when they returned. Once everyone arrived for the party, the three of us became the center of attention. I would sob once in a while but overall I was pretty happy, as was Cecilia. Daniela, however, fought with Julia, Negra's little girl, and bit her. We ate empanadas and pizza (I also got a taste). It's pretty late now and getting cold. Silva, Mariel and the entire family were here a while ago. Cuqui also came... I am going to go to bed early, otherwise I will lose my spot since there are tons of people staying the night: all of us, Elena, the fiorellas, Aunt Josefa, Aunt Hilda, and Uncle Poroto. Anyway, an entire army (I really don't like this word). Uncle Bachi, Chary, Inés, and Carolina went to get the cake and have yet to return. I want to touch the flowers and decorations but they stop me. I am thinking I am going to go to bed, tomorrow will be a very busy day.

Saturday 13

It's almost 11 p.m. and I am very sleepy. I would go to sleep but I really wanted to write everything down. Before 8 this morning Cecilia, Daniela, and I were gearing up for battle and ready to party. It was a beautiful blue sky day and everyone worked together to tidy up the house. At around 10, Chary started bathing us one at a time. Elena dressed us while Ana ironed and ironed, putting the finishing touches on everyone's outfits: from the bride's to mine. At around 11:30 we started to leave for the church. Danie, Beatriz, Ana, Chary and I were the last to leave and we arrived exactly when Inés and Bachi were about to walk in. They both looked so cute and so happy! It was a simple ceremony. As the couple was leaving their friends waved them farewell. I stole a bunch of kisses. People were saying that the three children looked like princes and princesses. Lela and my aunts were so proud! We threw a great party at home. Even though there wasn't any baby food, we ate everything. I even had a sip of cider. I played with everyone. Many people looked at me and said: "How I wished Carmen and Alberto were here." I felt a bit sad and nostalgic. I thought of my parents sharing this wonderful moment and it broke my heart. Uncle Sebastián, Ernesto, Elena, the Fiorella girls, Chary, Ana, Daniela, Beatriz, Bachi's parents, Elvira, Zulema, and I left at around 10 p.m. to take the newlyweds to Ayola street. We were bundled up because it was getting colder and the wind was picking up. Once they got on the bus we followed honking until they reached the Uriburu stop a few blocks further. Now, as I said, we have returned home. My cousins have left and Ana is playing with me. The party has ended and the house is quiet. Congratulations to my aunt and uncle!

Thursday 18

My "annoyance," which started on Monday, has lasted a while. I am better today. I have learned two things in this period of time: Lela brings me close to the doors and I move the latch and open them. I also put the rubber duck on my head and it makes me laugh so I do it all the time. "Let's see what mama's boy does with the duck?" — my aunts and Lela say, and I start the game again. I am also getting another tooth. I chew hard and grind with the teeth that I already have. My aunts say that Mom used to do the same... I am watching T.V. I like Petete[22] and the commercials featuring babies... I want to crawl around in the backyard but it's cold. It's getting dark and the round, beautiful moon is approaching. Chary shows it to me through the glass of the sliding doors. I "touch" it and laugh. "Luna, lunera, cascabelera..." She sings. I send it a kiss because the reflection of the moon will carry it through the windows of Mom and Dad's cells and leave it with them.

Wednesday 24

We left for Coronda, early as usual. It was still dark so I slept the entire trip. I was restless anyway because I was going to see Dad. He seemed well and was delighted with my new tricks. I showed him everything I had learned and even stood up by myself by the gate. Dad and Lela laughed because one of the guards took a liking to me and gave me a cookie. On the way back from the jail I saw cows and horses. I looked in awe and wanted to touch them. Once in a while I turned my head to look at the place where my father was. Chary

---

[22] A penguin that was a popular children's character.

made me wave goodbye with my hand. There was a lot of wind so my wave would have gone through the bars over the windows and reached my dad. I am sure that on his way to his cell he is thinking of Mom, of me, of the sun, of the beaches where he would like to take me on walks, and of that big blue world of freedom.

Tuesday 30
Today's is Inés' birthday. She is here in the house. We celebrated with cake. Lela showed off with one made of mayonnaise and rice.

Wednesday 31
A new trick: I went up two steps on the stairs. When they finally noticed, Lela ran to get me down but she changed her mind and let me walk halfway while she watched closely. Chary and Cecilita watched from the terrace. Such joy! I am growing so much! I can hardly believe it, I am turning one year old soon. I learn to live surrounded by love. I am no longer a baby. I am a mischievous little boy who wants to start walking to discover new things with each step.

June. Monday 5
We returned around midnight. I went to visit Mom on Saturday and Sunday. I was so happy! She found me big, all grown up.

Friday 9
Today I felt like crying so I did for a long while and I don't know why. But then I got a letter from Mom and I felt happy. She knows how to put an end to my bad mood.

Hello Gabriel!
Hello my love! Hello mischievous boy!

You know? I am happy because you came to visit and we were able to play and sing and laugh.

Tell me Gabriel, do you like getting letters? I put the letters in a box and when the mailman comes and says: "This letter is for Gabriel from Carmen!" Then he puts the letter on the train and then...riiinnn... a letter from Mom for Gabriel!... Hello Gabriel, do you know? I write one, two, three, many letters because I love, love you to the sky.

Bye Gabriel, my life.
Kisses, kisses, kisses, Mom.

Saturday 10

Today was my first misdeed: Lela took me to the corner fruit market and what did I do? I returned home with the grocer's pen!

It's 1:30 in the afternoon. We've had lunch and I don't want to sleep. Aunt María brings me to the back to get some sun and keeps me entertained by making play with the leaves from the orange tree.

Sunday 11

It's almost 7:25 in the evening. Ana and I just got back from Las Parejas. I'm wearing a pair of shoes that uncle Bachi gave me and I walk around while dragging the white chair from the foyer. I had lots of fun at Aunt Inés' house. I went all over town. I even went to the town square! And I played so much that I didn't want to leave. My uncle Sebastián had just left when we got back. He waited all afternoon for me because he really wanted to see me and tell me that he got a beautiful letter from Mom. Now I am very sleepy and I am going to bed. See you tomorrow.

Saturday 17
We woke up early. It was very chilly. We traveled to Buenos Aires with my aunts Elena and Chary. There were two girls on the train who played with me. When we arrived, the sun was shining and it had warmed up a bit. We went to see Mom. She was happy to see me and I showed her lots of tricks. I jumped with happiness so much that I am now exhausted.

Wednesday 21
I saw Mom again and showed her my new skills. I knocked on the glass a lot and cried a bit too. We went back to Aunt Josefa's house and I was so tired from playing with Mom that I slept the entire bus ride. I have a very bad cold and Aunt Josefa pampers me a lot.

Sunday 25
Argentina won the World Cup. Aunt Chary took me all the way to San Martín to watch cars parading and honking their horns and people singing in the streets. What mayhem! I kept saying: NTINA! NTINA!

Tuesday 27
I am sick. Cecilia is playing doctor and Daniela takes care of me. Today, Lela showed me pictures of Mom at her wedding and I recognized her!!

Thursday 29
A letter from Mom arrived with a colorful butterfly. My cousins and I stopped playing and we fought a lot because we all wanted to "read" the letter.

Hello Gabriel!
Hello my boy! You are so big now!
You know, Gabriel? I am happy, happy, very happy... Can you guess why?... because you came to

see me. Do you remember when I tied and untied my hair? And when we sang Hush Little Baby? And when I tickled your fingers? You know, honey, I love you so much that when you come to see me my heart beats faster, like the wings of a butterfly when it flies around the garden. I am sending you a butterfly and with it a piece of my heart that says: I love you, love you to the moon and back. One day I will leave here and we will take walks and ride the merry-go-round.

Bye Gabriel, kisses and more kisses for you, Mom.

July. Tuesday 4

Today I took my first steps with the help of Lela and Aunt Ana. They stood me up by the railing and called to me. I am not very steady yet but I am sure I am going to learn fast because I like walking on my own.

Sunday 9

They celebrated my birthday today at Aunt Isabel and Sofía's place. There was a cake with candles and lots of noise. They sang "Happy Birthday" to me. The Fiorella girls and I had lots of fun. We returned home pretty late and Aunt Elena and Chary were desperately trying to keep us awake since we are getting too heavy for them to carry.

Tuesday 11

Today is my birthday! My first birthday and I got a beautiful gift early this morning: a letter from Mom with a mobile she made to hang over my bed. It's a merry-go-round with horses and cars. This is my first birthday gift and I am very happy. Aunt Elena made a cake, put a candle on it and my cousins helped me blow it out. Enzo stopped by and took me for a ride in his truck. Then I went with Aunt Chary to buy pizza. So exciting!

Hello Gabriel!

Happy birthday my darling! How I wish to be with you, helping you blow out your first candle! Last night I dreamt that you were in my arms again, like when you were a newborn and I had eyes only for you. I wish I could hug you and hold you against me, caress your curls, feel your hand searching for my mouth, hear your hoarse laughter and happy squeaks.

Gabriel, I give you this merry-go-round and invite you to take a ride... Will you join me? Look Gabriel... Here is the horse... here a car ... and here a plane... Now, we blow on it and they go round and round! Do you like it Gabriel? I also send you a heart filled with kisses and my pampering. I love you lots, lots, looooooots, Mom.

Thursday 13

I have no desire to eat. It's raining. Chary took me with an umbrella and everything to order the cake for my birthday party. My birthday cake!

Sunday 16

My birthday party! There are so many children, gifts and balloons! My cousins helped me blow out the candle. Everyone clapped. I was so happy during the party! I laughed over anything. It was a great party and they took many pictures of me.

Monday 17

Though a bit late (Lela told me that Dad had been punished), I got a beautiful letter from him filled with dwarfs.

Hello son:

Happy birthday, Gabriel! Here is a gift for you. Do you know who these dwarfs are? ... no?... Well, these are the ones who brought your nail to my room, remember? Yesterday, they got out, got on the desk where I write and said to me: "We want to go visit Gabriel." Of course I said that they could and they got into the envelope and went. They live under the bed where I sleep. I am going to tell you the pranks they pull: they hide my shoes, they tear my socks, they make noises at night, they take the blanket I use; all this they do and more. They also eat cookies and make this cri, cri, cri noise... See if you want to keep them for a few days, but be careful... as soon as you turn your back they start misbehaving. You have to give all five of them names and then tell me. Don't forget!

I am going to go now. A kiss for you and another for Mom (did you give her the kiss I sent with you the other day?). Bye barrigón,[23] take care of the dwarfs and don't let them get hit by a car.

Bye, Dad.

Tuesday 18

Aunt Ana took me to her school. The children surrounded me and made me play a lot. There was so much sun! I crawl all over the backyard and on my way I would pull a leaf or flower from Lela's plants. I like to hold on to the railing and walk but sometimes I get scared and start to pout so Lela runs over to comfort me.

Monday 24

These past few days have been really hard for me. I got sick on Thursday. Oscar, who was studying with my Aunt Ana, took me to the doctor in his car. I had to be admitted because I had a high fever which went away all of sudden, but then I was shivering, had chills, and felt terrible. I spent all of Friday, Saturday, and

---

[23] A common nickname for children. Lit. "big belly."

Sunday taking medicine. Lela and Aunt Ana and Chary didn't know what to give me and pampered me all the time. Though I was only in the hospital until Saturday, I received tons of visitors. My cousins gave me tons of hugs and Aunt Elena carried me everywhere. I am better now, luckily!

Friday 28
It turns out I was not feeling that great. I have been indoors these days. Lela, of course, made me wonderful meals and I ate them. She made puree, meats, rice soup, juices... Today I started my mischief again. I opened the kitchen drawers and dumped everything on the floor. Lela laughed and then said: "Gabrielito, we have to collect everything and put them back!" I did exactly as she said!

August. Friday 4
I went to see Mom. I hate being searched! I cry a lot because they take off my diapers, away from Aunt Chary.

Saturday 5
Today I played a lot with Mom but, since the glass was bothering me, I gave it a good punch. Then we returned to Rosario. I cried a little during the trip back because I missed Mom.

Monday 7
Gabrielito, the pretty canary that Leli gave me, flew away. I wonder where it went, happy to be free?

Wednesday 9
A letter from Mom!

Hello Gabriel!

Hello darling! Tell me, did you take the train back to Lela's house?

Do you know, love? I now miss you a lot. I miss when you came to visit and we talked and played with the identification badge. And then I tickled your fingers from behind the glass. Gabriel, do you remember "Pulgarcito, Pulgarcito, Where are you? Where are you? I am here, here I am. Now they greet each other, now they greet each other, and they leave, and they leave?"

Gabriel, I love you to the moon and back. I want to be with you so we can play and I can help put you to bed. Bye, my love. I'm sending lots of chocolate and caramel kisses your way, Mom.

Wednesday 16

I have been too lazy to write. The thing is, I play a lot and by the evening I am too tired. I also watch TV and know the songs from the commercials. Today my cousins and I played way too much. We made the most of this beautiful spring day. In the afternoon, Uncle Sebastián came and took Daniela and I on a bike ride around the backyard. When he had to leave, I started crying like crazy. Good thing Natalia was out in the streets and consoled me. We ate bread dipped in milk and Nesquik. We played with balloons that Lela blew up. I pulled Daniela's hair and tried to take Cecilia's (who had just woken up from her nap) pillow.

Saturday 19

It's cold. Lela and Elana took me for a walk around a couple of blocks this morning. It's 8:45 p.m. now. I am playing with a jug. Once in a while I go to the TV and ask for tetete. I eat french toast and pretend to choke and when Aunt Chary says "ah!" I laugh. I put one of the horsies to bed and Lela rewards me with a kiss!

Sunday 20

It is a beautiful sunny day. I learned to play the piano with two fingers and I also sing. I also touch the stove and everyone says "TUTO!"[24] It's 8:58 p.m. now. I wear green pajamas and I am very sleepy. Ah, I almost forgot! Chary took me to the street this morning and I saw a car pulled by a horse. I wanted to touch it and kept saying: IEO, IEO.

Saturday 26

I walked on my own! We went to take a walk near the beltway with Aunt Elena and Chary, my cousins, and Uncle Ernesto. He made me walk. He kept saying: "let's go Gabrielito, let's go!" I laughed and clapped and everyone cheered me on. Afterwards, we passed by the zoo and the museum on our way back to Lela's house. I saw so many animals!

September. Saturday 2

Cecilia is sick and has been hospitalized. I heard my aunts and Lela crying. I think that she is very sick, but I don't know what she has. Everyone is very sad and worried. Mema (Zulema) took Daniela and me for a walk. The sun is shining brightly and it's warm. Spring is coming. Daniela and I play. I love it when people scratch my neck. They ask me "where does it itch?" and I say: "here."

Thursday 7

Cecilia is doing better and is home. I make faces so that she'll laugh. I learned to say Ca Ba Ca. I turn on the faucet in the bidet and I put my hands inside the toilet. I am a daredevil!

---

[24] This is a word used in Argentina to tell children that something is too hot to touch.

Sunday 10

Daniela and I get into such fights! I pull out strands of her hair. I mess up everything. I play with the wooden herb holder. Today I tried to throw it into the toilet! Everyone laughs because they say that I walk like Charlie Chaplin. I learned to play ball by myself in the backyard. My cousins came and we made a big mess.

Friday 15

Since Lela is in bed sick, I bring her my toys and tons of leaves. It makes her happy. I keep saying Ca B Ca and Te Te Te.

Monday 18

I traveled with Lela and Aunt Horacia to see Mom. First, I slept and then they made me play. I saw Mom. She was very excited. I told her all the words I know: Pa, CACA, TETETE, MAM. I will see her again tomorrow.

Wednesday 27

I have been visiting Mom these past few days. I returned to Rosario asleep. Uncle Moncho, Ernesto, Aunt Elena, Ana, and my cousins were all waiting for me at home. I was a bit drowsy at first but once I went around the house I was happy.

Thursday 28

I miss Mom. I'm in a very bad mood. I turn on the faucet in the bidet and crawl in. Lela gets upset because I get all wet. I point at the rose and say "uh" because it pricks.

Today is cleaning day and there is a bucket of water to play with. I stick my foot in it because I like to splash around. I put my hands inside and get all wet. Aunt Chary had to change my clothes. In the afternoon I went to Pablito's birthday party. I cried a little when they bathed me. Then I clapped because I was dressed in a white shirt and brown pants; party clothes. I took a balloon and some toys home. I liked the party.

October. Wednesday 4
A letter from Mom! Aunt Ana reads it to me and I clap.

Hello Gabriel!
My dearest boy:
I know it is difficult for you to understand this world with its gates and glass, of strangers who take you and change your diapers. I understand your outrage and tears. That's the reason I get exasperated when I see you suffer and there is nothing I can do about it from the other side of the glass. Today, however, my heart is happy because you definitely recognized me and know who I am. My eyes and my mind still hold on to the memory of your face against the glass, waiting, perhaps for a kiss or a caress from me. And I remember your tiny finger tracing my tears behind that damned glass.

One day, my son, I will get out of here and return to your arms. I will take you to the park and place you on the most beautiful horse on the merry-go-round and I'll blow kisses every time you go by me. I love you to the moon and back and I send you tons of kisses and caresses with each ray of sunshine that enters through your window, Mom.

Thursday 5
When the phone rings, Lela tells me "It's Aunt Chary!" I recognize the sound of the ringing and run as if I were going to answer it. It's raining a lot. My Aunt Inés and Uncle Bachi came to visit. They dressed me warmly and took me for a walk. Grandpa Donato came. I get along well with him because we play a lot together.

Sunday 8
It's a beautiful day because I got a letter from Dad. Also because my cousins came and we played all day.

Hello son:
It's been a long time! It's been a while since you have gotten a letter from me. But I always remember you and I want you to visit soon. Are you coming? Anyway, how are you son? I know it makes you laugh when I say that to you. But it's better than saying "barringón...barrigón, barrigón, gon, gon, gon... like a drum!

I played ball with my compañeros yesterday. Do you like playing ball? You will have to show me how you play when you come to visit. When I lived there I also played. Tell your Aunts to show you the pants, socks, and shoes I used to wear. When I was small like you... are you surprised I used to be small like you?... Anyway, I had a ball, too. But I will tell you all about it in my next letter.

I am going to leave you now. A big kiss for you and say hello to Luciana. Bye watermelon tummy, Dad.

Monday 9
The lilacs and lilies have bloomed. Daniela, Cecilia, and I play around the plants, causing mischief. I didn't want to take a nap so I scattered Chary's things all over the floor. Lela laughed, then told me that I had to learn to pick them up and place them where they belonged. I helped her. I played in the back with two worms while I ate cookies from Córdoba that Aunt Cherry gave me. I look at all the flowers. My face is covered in mosquito bites. Every now and again, the words MA MA escape my lips. We are not visiting Dad tomorrow because he is being punished.

Wednesday 11
I now have a molar! I said the whole word PAPA, and repeated it several times.

Monday 23
My gums hurt a lot, so I am irritable and cranky. Lela made me a sweet dessert out of cornstarch so that I would have some food in me and took me to the back to eat it. I thanked her by giving her tons of kisses and hugs.

Wednesday 25
I walk up and down the stairs by myself! Lela and my aunts hold their breath with every step! Lela spoils me too much. We are joined at the hip, Lela and I. In the afternoon we went to the Cathedral where there were other ladies like Lela. I walked around the pews while singing softly. Then I went off by myself to see the crypt. I gave Lela quite a scare because she didn't know where I was!

Saturday 28
Aunt Cherry watered the plants and I watched from the driver's seat of the car that used to be my grandpa's. I spend a lot of time there. I even turn on the lights. When I am taken out, I cry and kick. I played with Greta in the afternoon. I pretended to dump a bucket of water from the back and she ran all over the place. We sat in the doorway to the backyard and I pet Greta's head.

Sunday 29
I went to Aunt Inés' house. I had tons of fun. My uncle Bachi made me drive the car! We got back at night. I was so tired that I didn't even realize we had arrived home.

Monday 30
I learned to cut flowers. I say "Mom, Dad" to Lela and she understands me because I walk over by myself to a picture of my mom and dad and want to put flowers there.

I throw tantrums often. Today I threw all my toys in the air. I was given a saxophone and I am learning to play, or rather to blow.

November. Wednesday 1
I am going to have another cousin. My Aunt Elena came today and whispered that in my ear. I don't really know what it means, but I clapped.

Friday 3
I have discovered my pee-pee and use it to pee. When asked, I stand up and pretend to pee. Everyone has celebrated my new discovery.

On very hot days, I run around half naked and play with water. Stellita, Mom's friend, came this afternoon. I was in a foul mood and took advantage of the fact that Cuqui was there and threw a glass at her face. Lela gave me a good scolding and I cried inconsolably while holding on to the chair in the lobby.

Saturday 11
I traveled to Buenos Aires with Aunt Ana, and we went to visit Mom. She sang me our pretty songs and I moved my head from side to side. I was very angry because I had cried a lot while being searched. I then played with Mom but when we left I was a bit feverish. Aunt Josefa had prepared a nice soup and jello for dessert. I ate a lot even though I wasn't feeling well.

Monday 13
I "chatted" with Mom. She made signs with her hands and I, having climbed up on the parlor, laughed a lot. Then I played with other kids and got into a fight with one of them. I show Mom how I drink my bottle alone and she claps.

Monday 20
When the mailman comes with a blue or green envelope, I already know it is a letter from Mom. I hold it tightly and say, ma-ma-ma… Aunt Ana sat me in the high chair and, while I "destroy" the envelope, she reads Mom's letter.

Hello Gabriel!
Hello my darling! Do you know why your Dad and I can't go pick you up from Lela's house? Because they don't want to open the door to let us get out of here.
Gabriel, I want to be by your side and hold you and play with you. When they let us out, Dad, you, and I will go by car rides and eat ice cream.
I'm giving you this dog to sleep with at night. Tell Lela to fill it with sand. And make sure it doesn't fight with Greta! What are you going to call it?
I send you three woof-woofs with the dog and many, many kisses, Mom.

Wednesday 22
Today, Lela went to see Dad. She told me that he really wanted to see me. I listened to everything Lela was saying while saying PAPA-PAPA.

Friday 24
Since it is a pretty, sunny day, Lela took me to the corner to wait for Aunt Charry. When I saw her approach I started waving my arms and said "ta…ta…" I am good

friends with Greta. I walk around the backyard and she follows me. I pull leaves from the plants and throw them at her. It's hot and Aunt Ana lets me play with water. I took a nice bath.

They ask me: "where are your teeth?" and I point them out with my finger and laugh.

Tuesday 28

I don't want to sleep alone. I woke up in the middle of the night and went looking for my Aunt Ana. I cried a little and then fell asleep. When I woke up, Aunt Ana showed me something she had in her hands: a letter from Dad!

Hello son:

How are you barrigón? I am going to tell you a little story I thought of today. I woke up early because of a weird sound around my room. At first it sounded like the horn of a car... beep, beep, beep... but that was impossible inside a room. Then, it sounded like a cow...moo, moo... That can't be! I must be dreaming, I thought, and jumped out of bed. Can you guess what the noise was? No? It was music from a saxophone! And who was playing? One of the dwarfs! The little rascal was hidden under the bed, playing on and on. Do you know what he did when I got out of bed? He threw a shoe at me and ran so that I wouldn't be able to catch him and give him a good spanking.

I was very angry with the noise because it woke me up so early. So I decided to set a trap for him. I left a plate with a bit of honey and cheese (I know that this little one likes that) on the table and hid under the bench. I waited and waited and waited. Suddenly, I see a shadow on the wall tiptoeing forward slowly. He looked around and said: "Alberto is not here, I am going to take the honey and cheese..." And when he reached his hand to take it, I jumped out and said: "And what do you think you are doing, little rascal?...Are you going to eat honey so you have the energy to play the saxophone all night?... "No!" he shouted, and he jumped from the table and started running around... He jumped out the bed, then on the sink and finally onto the dresser. I chased after him. I caught him by the belt but it broke and his pants fell! He tripped and fell into the garbage can. I closed the lid, told him to stop, and then to tell me where he got the saxophone or I won't let him out. And do you know what he said? He said: "This is Gabriel's saxophone." "What do you mean?" I asked. "Yes," he said and told me his story: "When Gabriel sleeps, I take out the saxophone and play. Then, before he wakes up, I return it to its place." To which I asked: "Why do you do that instead of asking him to lend it to you? He is very nice and would gladly let you play with it." "Ok, next time I will ask him and I am also going to ask him to teach me to play some notes because he knows some," he responded.

Anyway, barrigón, this is the story that I wanted to tell you. I also found out something else... Do you want to know? The dwarf says that your tummy goes up and down when you play the saxophone and that it looks like a water balloon. Is that true?

Ok then, I am going to ask you when you come to visit, so try not to lie because I will ask the dwarf about it.

I look forward to seeing you in a few days, Gabriel. Give Mom a kiss from me and yank Cecilia's, Daniela's and Priscila's, and everyone's ears for me. Bye, Dad.

P.S. Do you like the penguin in the stamp?

Wednesday 29
I walk all the way up the stairs by myself! I took advantage of the fact that I can climb the stairs and went upstairs on my own. It scared Lela to death.

December. Friday 1
I said Ca-ca,-ca-ca. Aunt Ana took me to the bathroom and I pooped. Everyone was so happy.

Wednesday 6
It was very hot today. We left early with Aunt Chary for Coronda. When we got there, we were told that we couldn't see Dad. I didn't understand anything but I saw Aunt Charry arguing with some men. It was in vain. We went back to the bus station slowly and on the sunny side to wait for the bus home. Under the shade of a few plants, my aunt gave me a bottle and I slept. When I woke up we were already at the terminal. When we arrived I hugged Lela and gave her a kiss.

Thursday 7
A letter from Mom! I miss her so much and I can't wait to go see her. But I am a bit nervous and throw everything in the air. Just the other day I almost broke the television screen.

Hello Gabriel!
There is a little bird that stops by the window of my room and he told me that there is a baby I love whose name is Gabriel and cries a little whenever he has to take a bath. Is that true, my Gabrielín?

Let's see, do you want to play 'taking a bath'? Aunt Ana turns on the faucet and shissh, shissh... Look Gabriel! It's raining in the tub! And then, splash! We jump and get under the water. It's a wonderful shower! Now we close our eyes and the water falls over our face,

arms, tummy, legs and... oh, the water escapes through the grate.
Do you like the shower, Gabriel? Mom likes it, too.
Bye baby, I send tickles of rain to your eyes, Mom.

Friday 8
Today was the day of the Virgin Mary, and Lela took me to church. I kneeled on the pew, and then made a scene when I went up to the altar and "sang along" with everyone else. As we were leaving, a few women told Lela that I was very cute and smart. Lela was delighted.

Sunday 10
I traveled to Buenos Aires to see Mom. I do more and more tricks each time I see her and she gets very happy. My grandpa Donato was at Aunt Josefa's house and he played with me. Then he did something with his eyes, I don't know what it was, that scared me.

Wednesday 13
It's still hot. I wear a t-shirt. I look like a big boy. I got a letter from Mom along with a gift: a green horse that runs when I pull a string. I kissed it and then I played with the horse while Aunt Elena sang that pretty song that Mom used to sing. Since it's just me and Aunt Chary, I am getting into all sorts of mischief. She says that I woke up at midnight looking for Lela. I don't remember because I was half asleep.

Hello Gabriel!
Hello my love, my little firefly!
You know what, Gabriel? When you were little I sat you in the stroller and gave you apple slices while singing: "I have a green horse that jumps, brushes its teeth, rides a bicycle. It has a callus on its tummy from laying around on it, and when it goes into the river, it

turns around and comes out filled with colors. I taught it to talk and it neighs and it plays 'ta-te-ti' and can pee." Juan Marcelo, Martincito, and you loved that song about the green horse and laughed and blew bubbles with your mouths while I sang. I am sending you the green horse so that you can run with it around the backyard. Make sure Greta doesn't see because she will get jealous!

A kiss and a neigh, Mom.

Saturday 16
I ate puree by myself! It's very hot out. I played with Greta in the back with a bucket and lots of water. Then Ana drew a flower, a shovel, and a car and I pointed at them. I play with the ball and say GOL.

Tuesday 19
Aunt Chery reads me the beautiful letter Dad sent me while I try to put the buckets on my feet.

Hello son:
How are you, barrigón?

They told me that you were sick and they had to give you a "turkish bath" and medicine. They also said that your chest was making a sound like a grumbling accordion...

I hope you are better. You have to get better so that you are strong enough to run around and play the saxophone.

I would love to play with you but I can't. When they let me out to see you, we will go to the zoo, to the river, and there I will teach you how to fish. Would you be up for pulling a fish out of the water? You've never seen that? Well, you will do it with me. I have another surprise for you: tell me, do you like kites? It's a round thing, like a plate, made of paper and sticks and held together by a long thread. The wind takes it high in the air. You'll see, we will do tons of things together.

But I will have to keep sending you letters for now. Do you like the penguin with its baby on the envelope? When you visit we will talk about all these things. Did you get the letter with the story about the dwarf? You know Lela is there to read you everything. But I warn you… don't be causing troubles with your friend Priscila because I find out about everything!

Anyway, I will let you go. In a few days I will send you another penguin. Give your Mom a kiss when you go see her. I love you both.

Bye Gabriel, a big kiss, Dad.

Wednesday 20

Aunt Chary and I went to see Dad. He was very happy because I was fooling around and threw him kisses. He kept saying: "Gabrielito, Gabrielito" and I would wave my arms. I cried a bit when we had to leave.

Thursday 21

I climb on the couch, "dial," and "talk on the phone." I also dance to music.

Sunday 24

There is lots to do. Tonight is Christmas Eve. I am as mischievous as ever. I walk everywhere, turn on the faucet on the bidet, and throw toys into the air. My aunts and Lela are preparing something to eat for dinner.

Monday 25

It's Christmas! Aunt Chary called to us and said: "Baby Jesus came!" There was a mountain of gifts under the tree, things for everyone. My cousins and I didn't have eyes and hands wide enough to see and touch everything. They got dolls, necklaces, and many other things. I got a pair of pants, a ball, and other toys. The best gift was a letter and present from Mom!

We went to the river in the afternoon. We walked around La Florida and sunbathed. Then we went to visit Uncle Sebastián. When we got back, my aunts Isabel and Sodía were about to leave so we accompanied them to the bus stop. We came home and Lela had made me a delicious puree that my cousins and I ate in the middle of playing and jumping around with the ball. We went to bed early because we were exhausted!

My dearest:

Merry Christmas! Happy New Year!

Soon it will be a year since we were separated. Time goes by so fast! You have grown so much! You are now a big boy, running around the house and the backyard with Greta, playing with your cousins, and causing trouble. I have often wondered how much of our time together that tiny head of yours still remembers. But I keep those beautiful moments in my mind and in my heart, so that one day I can share them with you and give you back that part of your life and story. I was hoping for a miracle this Christmas. I was hoping they would give us amnesty and that we could all go home and see our loved ones, that I would hold you again in my arms like I have dreamt of doing since you were taken away. But the world is unfair. There is no place for miracles; the only thing we have is hope. We will have to keep waiting, my love. The day will come. There will be other Christmases and we will be with you, Dad and I. There is nothing I want more in this world than to hold you against my chest, look into your amazed eyes, and kiss your curls while telling you again and again that I love you to the moon and back. I send you this little car to play with your cousins, and the story of the traveling ant as a bedtime story for Lela to read to you. I send you many kisses with this moonlight that enters through your window tonight.

Bye my love, my little lion cub, Mom.

Wednesday 27

It's very hot. I have pharyngitis and am in a bad mood. The important thing is that I have new teeth, though! Teeth on top and on the bottom! Aunt Chary says: "Garbielito, let's see how you bite with your teeth." I pretend to bite her and laugh. How I am growing!

Thursday 28

It is so hot! We went to the Cathedral in the evening. I have been a few times but only now do I understand why people go: they have children or siblings who are in the same situation as my Mom and Dad; some of them don't even know where their loved ones are. They pray for them. I also "pray," running around the square, watching the birds, or wanting to climb the stairs to the post office. Being mischievous is also a way of praying for Mom and Dad.

Sunday 31

End of the year! How have I grown! I am exactly one year, five months and twenty days old. I walk, run, play with the ball. I have a lot of teeth and some molars. I can say: CACA, TETE, MEME, PA-PA, MAMA, PAPA, NENE, UPA, LELA, ICO and some other words. I am able to ask to use the bathroom (during the day, at night I wear a diaper… the shame!). I can feed myself, I try to write with pencils, I get into all sorts of mischief, and I like to take walks.

I am quite a little man!

Happy New Year, Mom and Dad!

Part Four
Toward Your Light, My Freedom

July 5, 1980

In a few more months it will be four years since that fateful day when my world stopped and gave way to the horror that has become my new reality. Since I was turned into a living witness of the pain of others and into a spectator of my own pain. I have spent four birthdays under these conditions, which is to say that years of productivity were lost behind these prison walls. Not everything has been lost, however, I have learned a lot here, mainly about living with others and about solidarity in the face of an annihilatory regime. I have met so many people! First, my great family in the Alcalidía of Rosario, then my dear *compañeras* here in Devoto with whom I've shared different cell blocks, some of them big enough to house 23 prisoners while others were too small to house four. Friends of misfortune, friends for life. Very few of them have been able to leave this place in the last few years but I have had the joy of seeing some who are very close to my heart be released: first Patricia with Martincito, and then Tere, Lala, Gladys, Mirta, and Marta. Later Cristina (leaving for Germany), and Alicia and Elenita (leaving for the United States). Many others, on the other hand, are still waiting for that decision that would allow us to pick up our lives from where we left them years ago. Mirta, Cristina and Violeta were my cellmates for more than a year. After being shuffled around in May of '79, I was taken to the fourth floor, to the cell that I now share with Griselda, Brígida and Patricia (Marta was here first but when she was paroled they brought in Brígida). They have been difficult years. There has been a lot of harassment, of reinventing oneself in order to survive, of unjustified punishment, of being taken to solitary confinement for simple things like asking where they had taken a *compañera* from our cell or getting too close to the window to see the rain or making Christmas cards for our families. Sometimes we were made aware of the new prohibitions when a few of us were unexpectedly punished for breaking them, like when we were forbidden from wearing flip flops to the yard or letting our hair down while in the visiting room. Everything is forbidden here; we can't be loud, we can't sing, we can't climb on the bunk beds to look through the window, we can't exercise, we can't do crafts, we can't wake up or sleep before the sound of the whistle, we can't do ANYTHING. If it was up to them we would be looking at the ceiling from 7 in the morning to 10 at night, waiting for food, the mail, and to be called to the visiting room (when we are not being punished). And it's true that the routine of being in jail becomes part of your daily life but we are rebels and do EVERYTHING that is not permitted. We look through the window, we exercise, we sing, we talk to *compañeras* in the adjoining cells while using the sink, we do crafts and make Christmas cards for our families too. Those of us who have children also send them letters with drawings and other things we make for them (and we paint the letters and the envelopes with beet juice or leftover tea or Mate leaves so that the little ones can distinguish them when they arrive). Nothing is done without a cost, though. Many of us have paid dearly with being confined to our cells or being sent to isolation for 10, 15, 30 days at a time.

Representatives from the Organization of American States were in Argentina last September. They met with families of the disappeared and the families of those incarcerated in different parts of the country. They also visited some of the penitentiaries, including Devoto. They promised to investigate the thousands of disappeared and, even though it pains us to know that this promise arrived too late (people started disappearing before March of '76), we take comfort in the fact that the existence of those made to disappeared has been recognized and given a place in our society and, hopefully, in the world. The OAS concluded that yes, there are people who have been made to disappear.

With respect to the rules at the prison, they agreed that these are too harsh; that they can't deprive us of healthier foods. They also can't deprive us of news from the outside world. The members of the OAS asked that we be weighed routinely and insisted on better nutrition, which resulted not in any improvement to the meals the prison provided us with but simply a wider variety of what was available for purchase in the prison store (mostly fruit, something we had not seen in years). Furthermore, and following the proposal to end our isolation, it was requested that we be allowed to buy newspapers and certain magazines. And something else new: there was a request that family members in different prisons could communicate with each other. The government approved these demands, which made us happier than we had been in a while. We didn't know, however, that we would pay for these benefits. They have decreased the indoor recess time from 5 to 3 hours and the extra hour of outdoor recess now mostly coincides with the indoor recess, which means we are usually only out of our cells for a total of 3 hours. This has hit us hard; we would have preferred to forgo the fruit for those extra few hours that were so important for our mental health. We have, however, also become stronger. We try not to stress over things and take the new measures calmly, without losing our positive outlook and faith. The heat wave that hit the region in March killed a number of people right on the streets of Buenos Aires. Even though the OAS demanded better conditions for us, we were not allowed to have our cell doors open (in Devoto these are made of wood and steel, making them heavy and airtight), even after two of us became dehydrated and had to be taken to the hospital.

There are still many of us here. After the mass transfers from the local prisons in '77, there was another transfer from Córdoba. There were about a thousand women here by the time the last of us arrived. Very few have been paroled or given the option to leave the country, so this prison is still pretty full. There are 5 floors of individual cells with about 93 prisoners on each floor. There are also several large wings with 23 prisoners each on the second floor of another building.

I have been in every one of the spaces reserved for the political prisoners: the prison nursery, the large halls on the second floor, two of the floors in the building with individual cells, and the solitary confinement cells. I have also been to the hospital. I was there for about a month after dislocating my knee while doing yoga under Yeya's direction—the same knee that had been dislocated during the torture sessions during the first days of my kidnapping. Those days in the hospital, shared with women I didn't know but with whom I have become great friends, have been unforgettable for me. It was also such a memorable time because it was the first time in over a year that I was able to touch my son. Furthermore, the guard had a moment of weakness when I started pleading with tears in my eyes to be allowed to hold my son. She gave me a minute. I crossed the gate and held him again in my arms.

I have lived through a lot, and very intensely, in this time of silence behind bars. I have grown a lot too. I have grown in my convictions, in being able to tackle this painful routine, in the knowledge that I am able to defend myself against the aggression of others, and in my capacity to patiently wait for this story to end. It hurts to know that there are many, like Marisol, whose whereabouts are still unknown. I don't know if they will return or if I will see them again. I also don't know what the city that I love so much will be like, if I am one day able to walk freely through it again. I wonder who I will run into on those familiar and well-traversed streets, and who I will never see again. The idea of freedom has become a double-edged sword for me. Though I wish for it with all my being, I am scared that I won't recognize myself in a landscape that no longer belongs to me.

It's been almost ten months since the Court of Appeals acquitted me of any guilt and of all charges. They didn't find me innocent, though, but they couldn't obtain any evidence to convict me for any of the crimes outlined in the 20840 Law on National Security. I was instead charged with breaking the 21223 Law on Ideology. I was convicted and sentenced to five years in jail and barred from holding public office ever, simply for thinking! Of course they don't like the way I think. The fact is that this law has been questioned by the International Court, which stated that every person has the right to think whatever they want because only actions, not thoughts can be punished by law. I took the opportunity to point out the illegal nature of a case that had for the defense attorney the same person who had been the prosecutor in the previous case. This didn't leave them much room to reconfirm the conviction, so I was acquitted.

But I am still under the PEN, as I have been from the beginning of my arrest and throughout this judicial procedure. So when Lieutenant Colonel González Roulet came in April to see "his people" (those prisoners under the jurisdiction of the 2nd Army Corps) I asked him why I was still here if the Court of Appeals had declared me innocent of all charges. His answer left me very confused: "I can't tell you what I think because I don't want to give you any hope." I didn't believe him because I was used to broken promises.

My situation has however changed for the better. A few days ago, another commander of the military came to see me. He was a huge man, dressed in an all olive green uniform and riding boots. I was not the only one summoned for this interview with him, there were a few of us from the 2nd Corps. With a look of disgust, like someone who was sure he was doing the wrong thing, he gave me a form to complete. It was an application for parole. After an initial back and forth over my desire to return to my old job teaching literature, and his insistence that this would never happen, I filled out the application to avoid losing this opportunity. So I completed the "occupation section" with "housewife" instead of the original "teacher." He told me that I would be notified of the outcome in July and that it was just as likely to be approved as be denied, so I shouldn't hold my breath. The other women who came to meet the commander were giving the same application, though only half of us would be paroled. The other half would be given the option to leave the country. I know that Marta, who was sitting next to me, was happy at the prospect of being released. However, deep down she would have rather had the paroled, and stay in this country, than the going away option that was given to her if she were approved.[25]

And that is how I got here. I feel strong, but I think it will pain me greatly if my expectations are not met. I have not been able to stop them. I can't stop thinking about restarting my life, free, with my son. The images

---

[25] The Right of Option to Leave the Country during the State of Siege. Even though it was one's right and one could opt to leave the country instead of being behind bars, it was difficult for relatives to get visas from other countries, which was the condition to be able to request that option. According to Sillato, the majority of these cases were denied. In the author's case, she had been given the visa by the Swedish Embassy but her option request was denied.

are so vivid of going back to my childhood home after all this time, being able to hug and kiss my mother, my sisters, everyone waiting for me out there, that it is impossible for me not to see them. On the other hand, it breaks my heart to think about the *compañeras* I would leave behind in this somber place of endless waiting and continuous deprivation.

It's the beginning of July and, if they do make a list of those who are to be freed, they would probably publish it around this time to celebrate Independence Day. My fate will be decided soon.

July 6

We were taken to the yard very early today. There are three of us from my floor who are waiting for the news that we have long been dreaming about. When we returned to our cell block there were two copies of the newspaper *La Nación* in the first two cells, one on the left and the other on the right. That is how the newspaper regularly made its way down the rows of cells.

We went back to our cells in silence but just a few minutes later there was a commotion and then the two soft knocks on the walls that informed us: the long awaited list has been published! In the blink of an eye the *compañeras* in the first few cells have started calling out the names of those who appear on the list. As the names travel down the row of cells, shouts of joy here and there could be heard. The guards turn a blind eye and for once let us celebrate.

I patiently wait for my name, convinced that I am on the list. But fate has something else in store for me and my name is not called. I slowly break down while Griselda, Brígida and Patricia try to tell me that there must have been a mistake, that they might still let me know later. Griselda then goes over to the sink, knocks twice and asks our neighbors to find out if my name is on the list. The answer arrives immediately: "Yes, of course, we thought we had said all the names." The stress of the last few minutes thwarts any celebration on my part and, contrary to how I always assumed I would react, I feel a big void inside and start to cry. The others think that I am crying with joy, but I am not. My tears come from a strange mix of joy, anxiety, pain, and guilt. It hurts me that these three *compañeras* who are now celebrating my good luck are hurting deeply, as I have been many times, because they are not the ones on the receiving end of this good news. Every one of these women I'll leave behind when I depart hurts. Through it all, I can't say that I am not dazzled by that word: paroled.

July 18

Today was our cell's turn to do the *fajina,* which is the cleaning of the entire cell block, except for the individual cells. *Fajina* day could mean either a very relaxing day or a total nightmare for those doing it, depending on who is on duty that day. The work is simple and when it's our turn we try to make it last as long as possible: cleaning the showers, mopping the floors, cleaning the only bathroom. We also have to hand out every meal to each cell. If the jailer is nice, it can be a wonderful day because the door of the cell is left open all day and one can come and go throughout the cell block as one likes. If the guard is strict then every time a task is finished, we have to go back to our cell and the door is shut. Today's guard is Cuervo, who is in between but leans towards strictness. We have been able, however, to walk around the floor and she hasn't been watching closely to see if we were finished to lock us up again. All in all, a good day.

We have no news about our eventual release (the two other *compañeras* on my floor, the compañeras in other parts of the penitentiary, and I). It's 3:30 in the afternoon and tomorrow is Saturday, which means that we will be here at least until Monday. According to the new order, prisoners can only be freed at noon (this was after many reports that prisoners who were released at night disappeared). And of course, nothing happens on weekends.

This is why the arrival of two search guards at such an unexpected time arouses suspicions. It's been about 30 minutes since they opened the cell doors and all the *compañeras* are out for the indoor recess. Suddenly the hustle and bustle dies down and eyes are filled with expectation. One of the guards approaches the gate and yells out the names of those scheduled for release, adding: "Ready for transfer." I run to my cell in order to climb to the window and yell: "hasta siempre, compañeras," as everyone before me had done. But the guard has followed me to the cell and, as if reading my mind, doesn't allow me to do anything else aside from change clothes and get my bag (the one that the *compañeras* gave me for one of my birthdays made of pieces of the blue uniform). I hug Griselda, Brígida and Patricia with a broken heart and renewed hope. I kiss everyone I encounter on my way to the gate and when the three winners of this drawing finally reach the other side, we turn around, crying, raise our hands and say "Hasta siempre," which is the same as saying "Hasta la victoria."[26]

6:30 p.m.

We have been here for three hours going through the same bureaucratic procedures as the first day we arrived. Mug shots, fingerprints, forms, etc. There are

[26] "Hasta siempre" and "Hasta la victoria" were expressions included in the farewell letter that Che Guevara wrote upon his departure from Cuba.

about twelve of us, all being paroled to different parts of the country. This means that it has been a concerted effort by various military corps to clean up its public image. We are finally placed in double file to walk to the exit gate. Those who had yelled and mistreated us are now friendly and wish us well as we pass them. The big door opens and through the darkness that has fallen early this winter evening we catch a glimpse of a few people on the other side of the street. We cross the threshold and the hustle and bustle of freedom invades us. The blinding lights and deafening roar of cars whizzing by at high speeds, completely ignorant of the miracle that has befallen us. We feel like newborns in this reality that we are now struggling to face. Every time we take a step forward to cross the street we pull it back quickly because we have lost our depth perception and can't really judge how far we are from the passing cars. But there are families waiting on the other side and finally, like in a game of red rover, one of us takes that first running step and the rest of us take off after her. In the end we are on the other side, safe and sound. I don't turn around to look at the place I have been for three years because, despite my tendency to be a rather rational person, I am still a bit superstitious and someone told me once that if you look back, you go back. I clearly don't want to go back.

The families surround us anxiously. Only one of them is there waiting for his daughter, the rest are family members of those who are still inside. They found out about the release during the 4 p.m. visiting hour and are there to get the truth about their loved ones still on the inside. The bravest of our small group say goodbye and head to the bus station to start their journeys home right away. I would like to do the same because I can't stand to be without Gabriel for another moment, but I have family in Buenos Aires and I am sure that they will want to take me home to Rosario and take part in that reunion with Gabriel and my family. The man who is waiting for his daughter—I now know that his wife was disappeared while looking for his son, who was also disappeared—takes the rest of us to a bar on the corner to have a drink. None of us is hungry but we all have a cup of coffee to toast our freedom. I am able to call my cousin Beatriz on the public phone. My other cousin, Mario, has been coming around noon every day since July 9th, including today, but went home after we failed to appear at the scheduled time. Beatriz is in bed. She is pregnant and has to rest, so can't pick me up. She asks me to take a taxi and that she will pay for it when I get there. The kind man doesn't let me or the other remaining members of our group whose families are in Buenos Aires take a taxi and instead takes us in his car—his daughter included—and begins the house-to-house delivery. I am the first one since Flores is very close to Devoto. When I get to the house, I see this other man waiting at the door: it's Mauro, my cousin Daniel's father. He approaches and gives me my first welcome back hug. Beatriz is waiting inside. We hug and cry awhile.

8 p.m.
Daniel just arrived. There is a festive mood in the air; they don't know what to do to make up for my years of suffering. But I am still disturbed; a part of me is still inside with the *compañeras*.

I always thought that the happiness I would feel once freed would be indescribable, but I never realized that any drastic change, even for the better, requires a painful transition to the new reality. They make plans; they're used to being up late so they tell me that we will be going to Ezeiza, to Aunt Josefa's house, for dinner at around 9:30. Before that we will stop by and see Daniel's sister. Their joy is so great that I try to join them on this first day of breaking with my routine of going to bed at 10.

9 p.m.

Aunt Josefa, with whom I spoke as soon as I got to Beatriz's house, is waiting for me at the door and runs to the car to hug me. There is so much love and warmth in those arms! Dinner is already ready. She has made some of her favorite dishes, which taste like delicacies to me since I've been deprived of good food for so long. Before I eat, however, I want to call home and talk to Gabriel. I have put off doing this so that I could fully enjoy my reunion with my other family in Buenos Aires. But now nothing stands in my way. My hands shake as I dial the number and as I wait to hear a voice on the other line. "Chary?" She immediately recognizes my voice and starts crying. I am so happy to hear her voice and those cries are so full of life! Then I hear: "Gabrielín, someone wants to talk to you," and a sweet little voice says "hello." My son, my wonderful son, how many times I have dreamt of this moment! I am so emotional that my voice struggles as I promise him that I will be there tomorrow with him; that this time it's true and I will be able to take him in my arms, we will be able to play and I will take him to the merry-go-round. He doesn't answer, only listens, but I know that he understands and follows everything I've said attentively. Chary takes the phone and tells me that Gabriel has stepped away and is watching her intensely with amazement in his eyes.

July 19

We are ready to leave. Daniel and Aunt Josefa are going to take me to Rosario. Beatriz stays because she needs to continue to rest. It's only a four hour trip and I am overcome with anxiety. Before leaving Buenos Aires, we will go see my cousin Mario, Haydee and their children: Mariano, Diego and little María Eugenia.

I say goodbye to Beatriz and we start the journey. The brief visit to Mario's family has been emotional since Silvia, Haydee's sister, is still locked up in Devoto—I was on the same floor with her for some time—and for Haydee it has been like seeing her sister again. Mario was as lovely and attentive as always.

The trip to Rosario is fast now that there is a highway, but also because Daniel probably went as fast as he could to make the trip shorter. Between my prison stories and my family's gossip the trip felt shorter and before I knew it we were entering my dear city. It's almost 4 in the afternoon on this sunny Saturday in July. I squint as I look around, trying to match the places I see to the places I've kept in my memory for all these years. The city has not changed much physically, without a doubt it has changed less than I have. We start to pass Oroño Boulevard, then Ayolas, Maipú, and now we are only three blocks away from my childhood home!

From the street corner I see someone at the door. It's possible that they have been taking turns waiting for me at the door because it's too much of a coincidence that they would be there the moment I pull up. There is Elena with Gabriel in her arms. When the car stops, Elena walks to the door and opens it. With my heart in my throat, I put my feet on the ground and get out of the car. My son, my sunshine, is in front of me. I reach out my arms and, as if our two and a half years of separation vanished in an instant, he throws himself onto me and wraps his little arms around my neck. We stay that way as we walk into the house for my reunion with my mother, my sisters and brothers-in-law, nieces and nephews.

I hug my mother with Gabriel still in my arms. She caresses my head, like when I was a child, and kisses my face and hands with tears of happiness. There also wait Chary, Ana, Inés in her fifth month of pregnancy, the Fiorella girls holding on to Elena's legs, Ernesto with six month old Darío in his arms, and Bachi and Angelita.

This ancient house's long hallway, which I had traversed so many times and seemed endless to me, now looks much shorter. Clearly my vision and my memory are playing tricks on each other and this house had grown exponentially in my imagination in the past few years until I lost sense of its actual dimensions. There is a lot of happiness, commotion, and new emotions. I go through every corner of the house trying to find myself in the spaces where I spent my happy childhood. I see my bedroom, the dining room, the kitchen, the backyard and the garden with their pretty plants even though it's winter. My eyes are slowly adjusting to the memories and I am remembering myself in those spaces.

Gabriel doesn't leave my side. He has guided me throughout and showed me his new helmet, bike, flashlight. He stops suddenly and pulls on my sleeves and says: "Mom, are we going to the merry-go-round?" My eyes tear up and my heart fills with joy. My darling has not forgotten my promises! The familiarity with which he calls me "Mom," his hands seeking mine, this simple but meaningful request, all tell me that there has never been a true interruption to this dialogue of love between us. I pick him up and hold him against me once more. Some day, when you are older, I will be able to tell you and you will understand. Today, it's enough to know that despite all the obstacles, this long separation, and breaks in communication, together we have been able to defeat the silence.

Epilogue
Reason for Writing these Memories

March 5, 1981

Today I went to the Intelligence Center at the Police Headquarters for the last time to sign documents for my parole. It had become part of my routine, at first going every other day and then once a week. Ironically, I have had to return to the same place to which I was kidnapped four years ago. Needless to say, those who were there to receive me each week were the same people who worked there back then. Some of their voices sounded familiar, but it's difficult to identify them. I have performed this ritual rigorously. Despite the diverse emotions that these trips to the Intelligence Service awaken in me, I have never missed a meeting because I know of the consequences that such a small mistake can bring. I say that this has been my last visit because it was communicated to me that as of the February 27th, 1981, decree I have stopped being under the PEN's (Poder Ejecutivo Nacional/National Executive Power) oversight. That is, I am, as they say, free. However, who is going to free me of my sorrows, of my anguish?

It has been seven months since that day, when the doors of the Devoto prison were opened and I was thrown, without any warning or preparation, into a reality that I would not be able to recognize or assimilate. I have not been allowed to leave the city limits, I was never given the permit, so often requested, to visit Alberto in the Caseros prison in Buenos Aires. I have Gabriel, I have my family, and I have my good friends but I don't recognize myself here. Something is missing, something has changed forever. I am the survivor of a catastrophe in the middle of a city that doesn't see me, that doesn't know my suffering, that knows very little about me. I barely talk to anyone who doesn't know my history because I am afraid that they might look at me weird and marginalize me. I feel like I am being unfair because I really don't know if I will find understanding and solidarity or just rejection. I don't risk sharing my recent past with others. I am always alert. I know that I always have to survey the place—meaning, the people I run across—before baring my soul to them. I know that I won't find a job if I open my mouth, because for many it would be compromising to hire a "former subversive," especially because we are still under a dictatorship and no one wants to take those risks. Sometimes I walk around, seeking out familiar faces, *compañeros,* who will transport me back to those endless chats in coffee shops; to those invincible projects; those joyous times and challenges. But my city is deserted for me. I missed my compañeras in Devoto. I would like to share this sorrow, this loneliness, with them. Stella's arrival to Rosario—my former cell neighbor in Devoto—and later Marta's, have brought me a bit of that air we shared there for so many years, and our bond has been reinforced here. We have found support in each other to face this emptiness.

A path opens before me. On either side of that path I see the faces of those close to my heart, who have never abandoned me during my years of pain. I see strength in their eyes and the love from each of them penetrates me and gives me encouragement., They tell me that it is worth it to keep moving forward. Gabriel leads me by the hand and we walk together. He is my happiness in the present and also my hope for the future. We wait for his father together. I feel that the "see you tomorrow" I said to him on the day he was transferred to Coronda is near. I think about that day, I think about all of those who are still waiting behind bars for that word or order that will allow them to retake their path, as I am doing today. I think about those who are no longer here, as well as those who we have not heard from, and it hurts me. I wonder when justice will be served. When will we get answers to so many unanswered questions? I now understand that my silence offers no way out, that it is my obligation to keep the memory alive, that that is the only way to make sure that one day the mechanisms that made all this horror and outrage possible can be unraveled. Therefore my testimony. Therefore my words, my memory.

Appendix 1

1) Compañeras/compañeros detained-disappeared that I saw or heard during my stay at the Intelligence Service of the Rosario Police Headquarters:

MARIA SOL PÉRES-LOSADA (MARISOL). She began her political involvement in the Unión Estudiantes del Litoral / Unión Nacional de Estudiantes (UEL /UNE), and actively participated in the "Fight and Return" campaign for the exiled leader Juan Perón. She received a degree in Social Work in 1972 from the School of Social Work at the National University of Rosario. She was a militant of the Juventud Universitaria Peronista (JUP) and Montoneros. Marisol was kidnapped-disappeared on December 16, 1976. She was seen alive at the Intelligence Service of the Rosario Police Headquarters before her disappearance. Inés Sillato remembers her thusly: "She was a great friend, full of ideals. She was another sister to me. We shared everything and I remember laughing to tears at her witty comments. When she was in her fourth year of Civil Service she met Raúl Ameris (Pucho). He disappeared after the birth of Andrés in February 1976. The last time I saw Marisol was at the Iglesia del Carmen in July of that year. Andresito would have been around six months old."

In the photograph, Marisol is with a friend, Rolando Elías Adem, who was also kidnapped-disappeared two years earlier (photograph taken by Adem's wife, Susana Munarris).

ANALÍA TERESA URQUIZO was born in Alpachiri, La Pampa, on July 3, 1954. She moved to the city of Rosario to study Psychology at the National University of Rosario. She was an active militant in the Juventud Universitaria Peronista (JUP) and Montoneros, organizing at the university and the surrounding neighborhoods. A family member remembers her thusly: "Analía, like her brother, has had a big personality ever since she was little. She was always smiling. She loved family life and enjoyed the company of her friends, with whom she shared hours of music and long talks. A huge fan of Joan Manuel Serrat, she had all of his albums… When she would come back to Alpachiri—already a committed militant—she would teach the kids from the shantytowns how to read and write. Her *compañeros* knew her as Clara." She was assassinated on January 26, 1977 in Rosario. Her ashes were returned to her family two years later. She was 22 years old. (Taken from www.lapampa.

gov. ar/ddhh-rostros-de-la-memoria/164-derechos-humanos/desaparecidosddhhcat/5999-uzquizo-analia-teresa.html)

In the photograph, Analía is with her mother and her brother Mario Julio, also a militant of Montoneros organization. He was murdered on January 16, 1977 at the age of 26 in the city of Rosario. At that time Analía was being detained at the Intelligence Service and never knew the fate of her brother (photograph taken by her sister in law Norma Fremrich).

ROBERTO LUNA: Militant of the Peronist Youth who was nicknamed "Zapato". Roberto lived alone in a shantytown in the south of Rosario. He had no known family. He had been in and out of orphanages and reformatories throughout his childhood and teenage years, and at the time of his kidnapping he worked selling ice cream. They kidnapped him early in the morning of January 18, 1977. He was taken from the Intelligence Service to be executed on January 26, 1977, at dawn, along with Analía Urquizo and María Sol Pérez-Losada.

A court case from March 1978 listed him as "having died during a confrontation." (No photograph available).

MIGUEL ANGEL NICOLAU was born in General Pico, La Pampa, on December 14, 1941. A Third World Salesian priest, he was a proponent of the popular and committed church. He was fluent in 5 languages (Spanish, English, French, Italian and Latin) and gave History lessons to high-school students at the San José School of the Don Bosco Congregation. He also extended his pastoral work to the shantytowns of Rosario. Miguel Angel was a militant of the revolutionary Peronist Youth. He was kidnapped-disappeared by military forces in the city of Rosario on January 27, 1977, at 35 years of age. He was last seen in the clandestine Intelligence Services detention center at the Rosario Police Headquarters on Dorrego and San Lorenzo streets. (From Norberto G. Asquini, http://www.laarena.com.ar/caldenia-la_pasion_y_el_infierno-91033-1.html).

In the photograph, Miguel A. Nicolau (with the handkerchief around his neck) (provided by José María Budassi).

Militants of the organization Poder Obrero kidnapped on January 20, 1977, and assassinated at dawn on January 23, 1977:

Between dawn and midday on Thursday, January 20, 1977, seven students and militants of the Corriente Universitaria por la Revolución Socialista, the student branch of Poder Obrero, were kidnapped from various parts of the city and taken to the Intelligence Service at the Rosario Police Headquarters. There they were tortured for three days by Agustín Feced's gang. One of them was able to escape. Sunday, January 23, at dawn the rest were assassinated in a simulated chase and confrontation near Cafferata and Ayolar (now Uruguay) Streets. That area, in the southeast of the city, was plagued with warehouses and had few homes. The bodies were buried as NN in the cemetery of La Piedad, but two of them were never recovered. (January 17, 2007. Source: El Ciudadano http://www.viubuzaglo.com.ar/arqdhh/cafferata-y-ayolas.pdf - provided by Roberto Atencio):

SILVIA LIDIA SOMOZA: 22 years old, native of Rosario. Partner of Héctor Luis Fluxá. Psychology student.

HECTOR LUIS FLUXÁ: 20 years old, native of Santa Fe. Partner of Silvia Lidia Somoza. Architecture student.

MÓNICA CRISTINA WOELFLIN: 25 years old, native of Rosario. Medical student.

NADIA DORIA: 33 years old, native of Villa Constitución. Psychology student.

GLADYS BEATRIZ HIRIBURU: 20 years old, native of Santa Fe. Wife of Luis Enrique Ulmansky. Psychology student.

LUIS ENRIQUE ULMANSKY: 24 years old, native of Moises Ville. Psychology student. Employee of the Isrealite Commercial Bank of Rosario.

MASACRE DE CAFFERATA Y AYOLAS

LOS HECHOS

Entre la madrugada y la siesta del jueves 20 de enero de 1977, siete estudiantes militantes de la "C.U.R.S.", Corriente Universitaria por la Revolución Socialista, perteneciente a la organización política PODER OBRERO, fueron secuestrados en distintos lugares de la ciudad de Rosario.
Recluidos todos en el centro clandestino de detención, tortura y eliminación de personas que funcionaba en las dependencias de Investigaciones de la Policía de la Provincia, en la esquina de las calles San Lorenzo y Dorrego, fueron torturados durante tres días. De allí uno de ellos pudo escapar, y en la madrugada del domingo 23 de enero los otros seis fueron asesinados el las inmediaciones de las calles Cafferata y Ayolas en un simulacro de persecución y enfrentamiento.
Sus cuerpos fueron sepultados como NN en el cementerio de La Piedad y los restos de dos de ellos nunca pudieron ser recuperados.

Silvia Lidia Sornoza
22 Años
Estud. de Psicología
Oriunda de Rosario

Hector Luis Fluxá
20 Años
Estud. de Arquitectura
Oriundo de Santa Fe

Mónica Cristina Woelflin
25 Años
Estud. de Medicina
Oriunda de Rosario

Nadia Doria
33 Años
Estud. de Psicología
Oriunda de V. Constitución

Gladys Beatriz Hiriburu
20 Años
Estud. de Psicología
Oriunda de Santa Fe

Luis Enrique Ulmansky
24 Años
Estud. de Psicología
Oriundo de Moisés Ville

Appendix 2

This is a partial list of detainees in the Alcaidía of the Rosario Police Headquarters from mid-December 1976 to October 1977:

1. Herminia Acevedo de Fernández
2. Olga Cabrera Hansen
3. Liliana María Feuillet
4. Hilda Barth
5. Blanca Cuenca de Moyano
6. María Inés Luchetti de Bettanin
7. Elba Juana Ferraro de Bettanin
8. María de la Concepción García del Villar de Tapia
9. Stella Maris Hernández
10. María del Carmen Sillato
11. Teresita de Jesús Marciani de Márquez
12. Gladys Marciani de Casco
13. Tita Marciani de Gómez
14. Gladys Gómez
15. Marisa Crosetti de Scaglione
16. Mercedes Sanfilippo
17. Marta Rivoira
18. Carmen Lucero
19. Patricia Antelo
20. Azucena Solana
21. Ana María Ferrari
22. Alicia Quintanilla de Paoli
23. Elida Deheza
24. Graciela Porta
25. Norma
26. Nelly Bianchi
27. Carmen Ariza de Cutrona
28. Eva Ojeda
29. Angela (trabajadora textil)
30. Angela Ferroni

31. Liliana Ferroni
32. Mirta Castellini
33. Tomasa Verdún de Ortiz
34. María Luisa Quiroga

Children born in captivity

1) Cristina Inés, daughter of María Inés Luchetti de Bettanin.

2) Eduardo, son of Teresita Marciani de Márquez.

3) Juan Marcelo, son of Gladys Marciani de Casco.

4) Gabriel Alberto, son of María del Carmen Sillato.

Another child, Andrés, was brought to the Alcaidía with his mother Graciela Porta and spent a week there. Due to lack of medical attention, Tita Marciani de Gómez had a stillborn son in February 1977. Tita died later during surgery.

Appendix 3

This is an incomplete list of members of the Second Army Corps based in the city of Rosario; regular officers and task force members ("gang") of the provincial, federal police; and wardens of the Women's Alcaidía (made on the basis of complaints that are in the hands of human rights organizations).

Note: Some of those named in this list are mentioned in this testimony. Others are not mentioned but were active members at the time of my arrest and during my incarceration.

Abbreviations:

GT: Grupo de Tareas // Task Force (made up of regular members of any of the repressive forces and mercenaries)

AAA: Alianza Anticomunista Argentina // Argentine Anti-Communist Alliance (parapolice force created by López Rega during the government of Isabel Perón whose function was to kidnap, torture and execute left-wing militants and sympathizers)

CCD: Centro Clandestino de Detención // Clandestine Detention Center (where the kidnapped were taken, many of whom were made to disappear).

S.I. Jef.Pol: Servicio de Informaciones de la Jefatura de Policía // Information Service of the Police Headquarters.

GONZÁLEZ ROULET, Enrique Haroldo- Teniente Coronel- Batallón de Comunicaciones 121.

SORIA, Fernando-Teniente Coronel- Batallón de Comunicaciones 121- Responsible for the political detainees at the Rosario Police Headquarters.

FECED, CARLOS AGUSTÍN- Comandante de Gendarmería- Chief of Police in Rosario- (76-78).

GUZMÁN ALFARO, RAÚL HAROLDO- Chief of S.I. 76/77- Sheriff - Torturer - Kidnappings and assassinations. Died of cancer.

SÁNDOZ, HUGO DIÓGENES- "El Mono"- Chief of S.I. at the Rosario Police Headquarters in 77/78.

MACOTE - Police officer in Rosario - In charge of the detainees in the female section of the Alcaidía at the Rosario Police Headquarters.

ABAL, Nora- Guard at Alcaidía in Rosario

ALMEIDA, Carmen- Guard at Alcaidía in Rosario

ALMIRON, Victor- Prison doctor.

ALTAMIRANO, Calros Ulpiano - Caramelo, Lucho- Officer, directed the brigade of the GT at the Rosario Police Headquarters. Operations Chief in the kidnapping and execution of Conrado Galdame.

DE LUCÍA, María Rosa - Guard at Alcaidía in Rosario.

DE PAUL, Elsa - Guard at Alcaidía in Rosario.

FERMOSELLE, Julio - Darío - Cabo- Car theft section.

GASPAROTTI, Gladys - Guard at Alcaidía in Rosario.

GIANOLA, Héctor - El psicólogo; Beto - Officer, directed the brigade of the GT at the Police Station in Rosario. Torturer, implicated in the case of Los Surgentes. Brother of the Assistant Chief of Police in Rosario.

GIANOLA- Brother of the above. Assistant Chief of Police in Rosario.

GÓMEZ, Calor Oscar - Carlitos - Deputy Chief - directed the brigade of the GT at the Police Station in Rosario. Implicated in the kidnapping and assassination of and the rape of his mother, Juana Ferraro de Bettanin.

"JAPONÉS" "MONJE" - S.I. of the Police Headquarters in Rosario - Member of the G.T. there. Participated in kidnappings and "transfers"

- Participated in the raid of Leonardo (dead?) Bettanin's house

JOVITA- Guard at Alcaidía in Rosario and in Tribunales.

JUÁREZ, Laura- Guard at Alcaidía in Rosario.

MARCOTE, Mario Alfredo - "El Cura". Implicated in the case of "Los Surgentes"- Former

Seminarian who worked for the Archbishop of Rosario - Torturer and member of the GT of the Rosario Police Headquarters - used to rape the detainees.

HERRERA- El Mono- Member of the GT of the Rosario Police Headquarters.

MARTINO, Graciela - Guard at Alcaidía in Rosario.

MUSCARA, Susana - Guard at Alcaidía in Rosario.

LEIVA- "Kunfito"- Sargent.

LOFIEGO, José Rubén - "El Ciego", "Menguele"- Officer - Torturer - Participated in kidnappings and executions - Chief of Interrogation for the S.I. at the Rosario Police Headquarters - Unknown whereabouts, Assistant Chief of Operations of the Unidad Regional II - Worked at the clinic

LOMBARDO, Norma - Guard at Alcaidía in Rosario.

NAST, Julio César - "Ronco"- Officer of S.I at Rosario Police Headquarters.

PERALTA, César - "Pirincha"- Auxiliary Officer - Seccional 12 - Police Station 23. Still active. Officer of Funes Section - Member of the El Topo Gigio gang - Common criminal. Starting in 1974 exchanges his freedom to be part of the GT of the Rosario Police Headquarters.

De PILAR- Guard at Alcaidía in Rosario.

RAMOS, Norma - Guard at Alcaidía in Rosario.

RUAK, Mario - "Weiss"; "La Bruja"- Officer of S.I., Rosario Police Headquarters - Participated in kidnappings and executions.

SÁNDOZ, Hugo Diógenes - "El Mono"- Chief of S.I. at the Rosario Police Headquarters in 1977/78.

SYLVESTRE BEGNIS, Luis - Médico - Related to the governor of the Province of Santa Fe.

TUR, Jorgelina - Guard at Alcaidía in Rosario.

VERGARA, Ramón Rito - "Pelado", "Sargento", "Colorado"- Non-Commission Officer - Participated in operatives, kidnappings and executions. Implicated in the case of Luppo de Rodríguez.

VIVAS, Carlos - "El Gato"- "Vidal".

ZITELLI- Chaplain of the Rosario Police Headquarters - Located at the San Pedro Apóstol parish in Casilda.

Appendix 4

The Case of Díaz Bessone (ex "Feced")[27]
Monday, March 26, 2012
Never again: life sentence for Díaz Bessone and Lofiego Ricardo Robins.

The Tribunal Oral Federal Número 2 de Rosario[28] sentenced Ramón Díaz Bessone and José Rubén Lofiego to live in prison for crimes against humanity during the last military dictatorship in the area of Rosario. Another defendant, Mario Marcote, received 25 years. José Scortechini and Ramón Vergara's sentences were 12 and 10 years respectively. The survivors and relatives of those who passed through the clandestine detention center operating out of the former Police Station believed these were too lenient given the extent of their crimes. On the other hand, Ricardo Miguel Chomicki, a former Montonero militant accused of aiding the oppressors after being kidnapped, was acquitted.

The case "Díaz Bessone," known previously as "Feced," investigated the crimes against humanity committed against 93 people at the clandestine detention center out of the Intelligence Center at the former Police Headquarters in Rosario. This was the biggest one in the state and around 1,800 to 2,000 people are estimated to have passed through it. (Taken from www.rosario3.com/noticias/noticias.aspx?idNot=109056).

---

[27] 26 Sillato was one of the witnesses who testified in this case. She testified again in two more cases in 2014 and 2019.
[28] Similar to Federal District Courts in the US.

www.ingramcontent.com/pod-product-compliance
Lightning Source LLC
Chambersburg PA
CBHW030152100526
44592CB00009B/235